Minor Error, Major Consequences: True Stories of Unexpected Impacts

Shah Rukh

Published by Shah Rukh, 2024.

While every precaution has been taken in the preparation of this book, the publisher assumes no responsibility for errors or omissions, or for damages resulting from the use of the information contained herein.

MINOR ERROR, MAJOR CONSEQUENCES: TRUE STORIES OF UNEXPECTED IMPACTS

First edition. August 6, 2024.

Copyright © 2024 Shah Rukh.

Written by Shah Rukh.

Table of Contents

Prologue

In the annals of history, the line between success and catastrophe is often razor-thin. It is a line that has been crossed many times, not by grand blunders or monumental miscalculations, but by seemingly minor errors. A small oversight, a misjudged calculation, or a momentary lapse in attention can ripple outwards, setting off a chain of events with devastating consequences. This book is a chronicle of such moments—where tiny mistakes led to monumental disasters, forever altering the course of human history.

We live in a world that often celebrates the spectacular and the grand, but in these pages, we turn our focus to the subtle and the minute. Here, the spotlight is on the minor errors and oversights that unleashed forces far beyond their origins. Each chapter delves into a unique incident, dissecting how a small mistake spiraled into a major catastrophe. These are stories of human error and its unforgiving repercussions, where the difference between routine and ruin was a split-second decision or a fraction of an inch.

From the control room of Chernobyl to the iceberg-laden waters of the North Atlantic, from the skies over Tenerife to the molasses-filled streets of Boston, we journey through time and space, uncovering the intricate details and human stories behind each disaster. The tales in this book are a stark reminder that our world is a fragile web of interconnections, where the smallest thread, if tugged at the wrong moment, can unravel the entire tapestry.

As we explore these incidents, we also reflect on the lessons learned and the measures taken to prevent future occurrences. Each story is a testament to human fallibility and resilience, illustrating not only the catastrophic potential of small errors but also the indomitable spirit of recovery and reform.

"Minor Error, Major Consequences: True Stories of Unexpected Impacts" is not just a collection of cautionary tales; it is an exploration of the profound impact of our actions, however insignificant they may seem. It is an invitation to ponder the delicate balance of our existence and to appreciate the importance of diligence, precision, and awareness in every aspect of life.

As you turn the pages, may these stories serve as a sobering reminder of the unexpected power of minor errors and inspire a deeper respect for the complexities of the world we navigate.

Chapter 1: The Chernobyl Control Room Mishap

The Chernobyl disaster stands as one of the most catastrophic nuclear accidents in history, and at its core lies a series of seemingly minor errors that culminated in devastating consequences. On April 26, 1986, during a late-night safety test at Reactor No. 4 of the Chernobyl Nuclear Power Plant in Pripyat, Ukraine, a combination of design flaws, operator errors, and procedural violations led to an uncontrolled reaction. The mishap began in the control room, a space that was meant to be the hub of safety and oversight but became the crucible of disaster.

The safety test aimed to simulate a power outage, ensuring that the reactor could continue to be cooled even in the absence of electricity. However, several crucial mistakes were made in preparation for and during the test. The reactor was running at low power, a state in which it was unstable. Despite the potential risks, the test proceeded under these unsafe conditions. The operators were unaware of many of the reactor's design flaws, particularly the positive void coefficient, which could lead to an increase in reactivity when the coolant water turned to steam.

As the test commenced, operators made the critical decision to disable several safety systems, including the emergency core cooling system. This step was taken to prevent interference with the test, but it removed crucial layers of protection. The reactor's power output fell to near zero, and in an attempt to raise it, the operators withdrew most of the control rods, which regulate the reactor's fission process. This action increased the reactor's instability.

The control room operators, following their instructions, were unaware of the reactor's precarious state. The indicators and alarms that should have alerted them to the danger were either ignored or misunderstood due to insufficient training and the complexity of the system. The reactor's power surged uncontrollably, leading to a massive steam buildup. This steam production caused a significant increase in reactivity, creating a vicious cycle of escalating heat and pressure.

In a desperate attempt to shut down the reactor, an emergency button was pressed to insert all control rods back into the core. However, a fatal flaw in the control rod design exacerbated the situation. The rods had graphite tips that initially displaced coolant, temporarily increasing reactivity before the boron within the rods could slow the reaction. This design flaw, combined with the existing conditions, triggered a massive explosion.

The explosion blew off the reactor's 1,000-ton steel and concrete lid, releasing a significant amount of radioactive material into the atmosphere. Fires broke out, further dispersing radioactive particles. The immediate explosion killed two plant workers, but the subsequent release of radiation led to acute radiation sickness and death for many more, including firefighters and plant workers who responded to the disaster.

The mishap in the control room was compounded by the Soviet government's initial attempts to downplay the severity of the accident. Evacuations of nearby towns, including Pripyat, were delayed, leading to unnecessary exposure to radiation for thousands of residents. The lack of timely information and the failure to promptly mobilize emergency response teams magnified the human and environmental toll.

The long-term consequences of the Chernobyl disaster are profound. Vast areas surrounding the plant were contaminated, resulting in the creation of the Chernobyl Exclusion Zone, an area spanning 30 kilometers where human habitation is restricted. The disaster caused a spike in cancer rates, particularly thyroid cancer, among the exposed population. The environmental impact included radiation-induced mutations in flora and fauna, with some areas remaining uninhabitable for centuries.

The Chernobyl disaster also had significant political and social repercussions. It exposed the shortcomings of the Soviet Union's nuclear safety protocols and emergency response mechanisms. The global community's reaction, coupled with internal pressures, forced Soviet leadership to adopt more transparent policies. This transparency, though limited, contributed to the eventual dissolution of the Soviet Union as it revealed systemic inefficiencies and corruption within the government.

In the realm of nuclear energy, the disaster led to sweeping changes in safety standards and protocols worldwide. It underscored the need for rigorous training, robust safety systems, and transparent communication channels. The International Atomic Energy Agency (IAEA) and other bodies implemented stricter regulations and encouraged international cooperation to prevent similar incidents.

The control room mishap at Chernobyl serves as a grim reminder of how a series of minor errors and oversights can cascade into a monumental catastrophe. The event highlighted the critical importance of safety culture, the need for rigorous adherence to protocols, and the profound consequences that can arise from complacency and lack of preparedness. The lessons learned from Chernobyl continue to shape nuclear safety practices and emergency response strategies, aiming to prevent future tragedies of such magnitude.

Chapter 2: Titanic's Fatal Iceberg Oversight

The tragic sinking of the RMS Titanic on April 15, 1912, remains one of the most infamous maritime disasters in history. The catastrophic event resulted from a series of errors and oversights, culminating in the ship striking an iceberg. This seemingly minor navigational error led to the loss of more than 1,500 lives, highlighting the vulnerability of even the most advanced engineering marvels to the forces of nature and human fallibility.

The RMS Titanic, touted as the "unsinkable" ship, was a state-of-the-art luxury liner constructed by the White Star Line. It was the largest and most opulent ship of its time, symbolizing human ingenuity and technological prowess. The ship's maiden voyage from Southampton to New York City was highly anticipated, drawing passengers from various walks of life, including some of the wealthiest and most influential individuals of the era.

The seeds of the disaster were sown long before the Titanic set sail. The ship's design, while advanced, had several critical flaws. One of the most significant was the insufficient number of lifeboats. Although the ship was equipped with 20 lifeboats, enough for only about half of the 2,224 passengers and crew aboard, this complied with outdated maritime safety regulations. The lifeboats were intended more for ferrying passengers to rescue ships rather than providing sufficient capacity for everyone on board.

As the Titanic embarked on its voyage, the crew received multiple iceberg warnings from other ships in the vicinity of the North Atlantic. Despite these warnings, the ship maintained a high speed, partly due to pressure to make a swift crossing and demonstrate its capabilities. Captain Edward Smith, an experienced mariner nearing retirement, was confident in the ship's invulnerability and the crew's ability to navigate through the icy waters.

On the night of April 14, 1912, the Titanic sailed under clear skies and calm seas, creating an illusion of safety. However, these conditions made icebergs harder to spot, as there were no waves breaking against them to create a visible spray. Lookouts Frederick Fleet and Reginald Lee were stationed in the crow's nest, tasked with spotting any potential hazards. Unfortunately, they did not have binoculars, which had been misplaced before the voyage, further hampering their ability to detect icebergs.

At approximately 11:40 PM, Fleet spotted an iceberg directly in the Titanic's path and rang the warning bell three times. He immediately informed the bridge, where First Officer William Murdoch attempted to maneuver the ship away from the iceberg by ordering a hard-a-starboard turn and reversing the engines. However, the ship's immense size and speed hindered its ability to turn quickly. The starboard side of the Titanic scraped along the iceberg, resulting in a series of punctures along the hull below the waterline.

The collision, which lasted only a few seconds, caused catastrophic damage. The iceberg tore through the hull's iron plates, compromising the ship's watertight compartments. Although the Titanic was designed to stay afloat with up to four flooded compartments, the iceberg had breached six. The ship's fate was sealed within minutes of the collision, although it would take more than two hours for it to sink completely.

As water began to pour into the lower compartments, the crew and passengers were initially unaware of the severity of the situation. The Titanic's designer, Thomas Andrews, conducted a quick assessment and informed Captain Smith that the ship would inevitably sink. Captain Smith ordered the lifeboats to be prepared and sent out distress signals, hoping for a nearby ship to come to their aid.

The evacuation process was chaotic and poorly managed. Lifeboat drills had not been conducted, and many passengers did not realize the gravity of the situation until it was too late. Officers on the ship misinterpreted the "women and children first" protocol, leading to lifeboats being launched half-full. Additionally, language barriers and the lack of clear instructions exacerbated the confusion.

The closest ship to respond to the Titanic's distress signals was the RMS Carpathia, which was approximately 58 miles away. Despite racing at full speed, it took the Carpathia more than three hours to reach the sinking Titanic. In the meantime, the Titanic's crew struggled to maintain order and launch the lifeboats. Many third-class passengers were trapped below decks, unable to reach the lifeboats due to locked gates and the ship's complex layout.

As the bow of the Titanic dipped below the waterline, the stern rose high into the air. The ship eventually broke in two, with the bow section sinking rapidly and the stern remaining afloat for a few more minutes before plunging into the icy depths. Survivors in the lifeboats faced a harrowing wait in the frigid Atlantic waters, listening to the cries of those still in the water slowly fading as hypothermia set in.

The Carpathia arrived at the scene around 4:00 AM, rescuing the 705 survivors. The aftermath of the disaster sent shockwaves around the world, leading to widespread mourning and a reevaluation of maritime safety practices. The tragedy of the Titanic highlighted the need for improved lifeboat capacity, better training for crew members, and stricter adherence to safety protocols.

The Titanic's fatal iceberg oversight had profound and lasting consequences. The disaster prompted the establishment of the International Convention for the Safety of Life at Sea (SOLAS) in 1914, which set new standards for lifeboat availability, emergency equipment, and crew training. The incident also underscored the importance of humility in the face of nature's power, reminding society that no technological marvel is truly invincible.

The sinking of the Titanic remains a poignant lesson in the consequences of hubris and the critical importance of vigilance and preparedness. The convergence of human error, inadequate safety measures, and nature's unpredictability led to a disaster that continues to resonate more than a century later. The story of the Titanic serves as a solemn reminder of the fragility of human endeavors and the need to respect and anticipate the forces beyond our control.

Chapter 3: The Challenger O-Ring Disaster

The Space Shuttle Challenger disaster on January 28, 1986, remains one of the most tragic and consequential events in the history of space exploration. The loss of the Challenger and its seven-member crew, including civilian teacher Christa McAuliffe, was a profound national tragedy for the United States and a stark reminder of the dangers inherent in human spaceflight. Central to the disaster was a seemingly minor technical flaw: the failure of an O-ring seal in one of the solid rocket boosters (SRBs). This small error had catastrophic consequences, leading to the disintegration of the shuttle just 73 seconds after liftoff.

The Space Shuttle program, initiated by NASA in the 1970s, was designed to provide a reusable spacecraft capable of carrying astronauts and cargo to low Earth orbit. The shuttle's design included two solid rocket boosters (SRBs), a large external fuel tank, and the orbiter itself. The SRBs, manufactured by Morton Thiokol, were crucial for providing the thrust necessary to lift the shuttle off the launch pad and into space. Each SRB consisted of multiple segments joined by field joints, which were sealed with rubber O-rings to prevent hot gases from escaping during ignition and ascent.

From the outset, concerns about the O-ring seals were evident. Engineers at Morton Thiokol had observed that the O-rings were susceptible to erosion and could become brittle in cold temperatures, compromising their ability to maintain an effective seal. Despite these concerns, the design was deemed acceptable, with the assumption that redundancy (two O-rings per joint) would provide adequate protection.

In the months leading up to the Challenger launch, engineers noted several instances where O-rings had experienced significant erosion during previous flights. These observations prompted internal discussions and memos warning of potential catastrophic failure if the O-rings did not function as intended. However, the urgency of the warnings was not fully communicated to NASA management, and no decisive action was taken to address the issue comprehensively.

The Challenger mission, STS-51-L, was initially scheduled for January 22, 1986, but a series of delays pushed the launch to January 28. On the morning of the launch, temperatures at Kennedy Space Center in Florida were unusually cold, dropping to as low as 18 degrees Fahrenheit. Engineers at Morton Thiokol were acutely aware that the low temperatures could adversely affect the O-rings' performance. During a teleconference with NASA officials on the eve of the launch, Morton Thiokol engineers, led by Roger Boisjoly, strongly recommended postponing the launch due to the potential risk of O-ring failure.

However, under pressure from NASA management and senior Morton Thiokol executives, who were keen to maintain the shuttle program's schedule, the engineers' concerns were overruled. Morton Thiokol management reversed their initial recommendation and gave the go-ahead for the launch. The decision was influenced by a complex interplay of organizational, cultural, and bureaucratic factors, including a strong emphasis on maintaining the shuttle's launch schedule, which had already faced numerous delays.

On the morning of January 28, the launch proceeded as planned. As the countdown reached zero, the SRBs ignited, and the Challenger lifted off. The crew, comprising Francis R. Scobee, Michael J. Smith, Ronald McNair, Ellison Onizuka, Judith Resnik, Gregory Jarvis, and Christa McAuliffe, were embarking on what was intended to be a milestone mission. McAuliffe, a schoolteacher, was set to be the first civilian teacher in space, a fact that garnered significant public and media attention.

Approximately 58 seconds into the flight, a small puff of black smoke was visible near the right SRB's aft field joint, indicating that hot gases were escaping through a compromised O-ring seal. The cold weather had indeed affected the O-rings, causing them to become rigid and unable to expand and seal the joint properly. Despite this early sign of trouble, the shuttle continued its ascent.

At T+73 seconds, disaster struck. A flame from the breached joint in the right SRB burned through the lower strut that attached the booster to the external fuel tank. The SRB then pivoted around its upper attachment, causing the nose of the shuttle to twist. This movement ruptured the external fuel tank, releasing a massive amount of liquid hydrogen and oxygen. The resultant explosion created a huge fireball, and the shuttle was torn apart by aerodynamic forces.

The crew cabin, along with the intact SRBs, was seen emerging from the fireball, and both continued to ascend briefly before falling back into the Atlantic Ocean. It is believed that the crew survived the initial breakup, but the subsequent impact with the ocean at high velocity was not survivable. The loss of Challenger and its crew was broadcast live to a shocked and horrified global audience.

In the immediate aftermath, President Ronald Reagan appointed a commission, chaired by former Secretary of State William Rogers, to investigate the disaster. The Rogers Commission included notable figures such as physicist Richard Feynman, astronaut Sally Ride, and Air Force General Donald Kutyna. The commission's investigation revealed the direct cause of the disaster: the failure of the O-ring seal in the right SRB, exacerbated by the cold temperatures on the morning of the launch.

The investigation also uncovered deeper, systemic issues within NASA and its contractors. The commission's report highlighted a flawed decision-making process, a lack of effective communication, and an organizational culture that prioritized schedule and budget considerations over safety. Richard Feynman's famous demonstration during a commission hearing, where he placed an O-ring segment in a glass of ice water to illustrate its loss of flexibility at low temperatures, starkly underscored the technical issues that had been overlooked.

The Rogers Commission made several recommendations to improve the safety and reliability of the Space Shuttle program. These included redesigning the SRB joints, enhancing NASA's organizational culture to prioritize safety, and establishing better communication channels between engineers and management. The shuttle program was suspended for nearly three years as these recommendations were implemented, and significant changes were made to prevent a recurrence of such a disaster.

The Challenger disaster had far-reaching implications for NASA and the broader field of space exploration. It underscored the inherent risks of spaceflight and the critical importance of rigorous safety protocols and vigilant oversight. The loss of the Challenger crew served as a sobering reminder of the human cost of exploration and the need for constant vigilance and humility in the face of technological challenges.

In the years since the disaster, the lessons learned from Challenger have continued to shape NASA's approach to safety and risk management. The legacy of the Challenger crew endures in the ongoing efforts to push the boundaries of human space exploration while striving to ensure that such a tragedy is never repeated. The Challenger O-ring disaster remains a poignant example of how minor technical issues, if not properly addressed, can lead to catastrophic outcomes, emphasizing the critical importance of prioritizing safety above all else in the pursuit of scientific and technological advancement.

Chapter 4: Hiroshima's Targeting Miscalculation

The atomic bombing of Hiroshima on August 6, 1945, stands as one of the most devastating events in human history. The decision to target Hiroshima was influenced by a combination of military strategy, scientific considerations, and, unfortunately, a series of miscalculations. The consequences of these decisions resulted in unprecedented destruction and loss of life, shaping the post-war era and the global discourse on nuclear weapons.

In the final stages of World War II, the United States was seeking a decisive action to compel Japan to surrender and bring an end to the conflict. Despite the Allied forces' advances, Japan showed no signs of capitulating, and the prospect of a prolonged and bloody invasion of the Japanese mainland loomed large. The Manhattan Project, a secret research and development initiative, had successfully developed atomic bombs, providing a potential means to force Japan's surrender without further extensive Allied casualties.

A committee known as the Interim Committee, comprising military officials, scientists, and government representatives, was tasked with advising on the use of the atomic bomb. They considered several potential targets, with criteria including the target's military significance, the likelihood of civilian casualties, and the psychological impact of the bomb. Among the cities considered were Kyoto, a cultural and historical center; Hiroshima, an industrial and military hub; and Nagasaki, another industrial city.

Kyoto, despite being initially considered, was ultimately removed from the list due to its cultural and historical significance. The Secretary of War, Henry Stimson, who had visited Kyoto and appreciated its cultural heritage, argued strongly against targeting it. This decision underscored the delicate balance between military objectives and the desire to avoid wanton destruction of cultural landmarks.

Hiroshima, on the other hand, was seen as an ideal target for several reasons. It was a major military command center, housing the headquarters of the Second General Army, which was responsible for the defense of southern Japan. Additionally, it had significant industrial facilities that supported the Japanese war effort, including factories producing military supplies and equipment. Hiroshima's relatively untouched status due to limited prior bombings also made it a prime candidate to demonstrate the bomb's full destructive capability.

However, the choice of Hiroshima was not without miscalculations and oversights. One of the key miscalculations was the underestimation of the bomb's destructive power and its impact on civilian populations. The planners were aware that civilian casualties would be significant, but they did not fully grasp the extent of the devastation that would unfold. This lack of foresight was partly due to the novelty of the weapon and the limited understanding of its long-term effects, such as radiation sickness.

Another significant miscalculation involved the weather conditions and the bomb's delivery method. On the morning of August 6, 1945, the B-29 bomber Enola Gay, piloted by Colonel Paul Tibbets, took off from Tinian Island in the Pacific. The primary target was Hiroshima, with Kokura and Nagasaki as secondary targets in case weather conditions were unfavorable. The bomb, nicknamed "Little Boy," was a uranium-235 gun-type weapon that had never been tested before in combat conditions.

As the Enola Gay approached Hiroshima, weather reconnaissance planes reported clear skies, facilitating visual targeting. The bomb was dropped at 8:15 AM local time, aiming for the Aioi Bridge, a prominent T-shaped bridge in the city center. The bomb exploded approximately 1,900 feet above the city to maximize the blast radius and destructive impact. The explosion created a fireball with temperatures reaching several million degrees Fahrenheit, instantly vaporizing everything within a 1,000-foot radius and igniting a massive firestorm.

The immediate impact was catastrophic. An estimated 70,000 to 80,000 people were killed instantly, with tens of thousands more succumbing to injuries and radiation sickness in the subsequent days, weeks, and months. The blast obliterated nearly five square miles of the city, destroying homes, schools, hospitals, and infrastructure. The intense heat and radiation caused severe burns and long-term health effects, including increased cancer rates among survivors, known as hibakusha.

The scale of the devastation shocked even those who had planned and executed the mission. The long-term effects of radiation exposure were not fully understood at the time, and the suffering of the survivors added a grim dimension to the immediate destruction. The decision to use the bomb, while justified by some as necessary to end the war and save lives that would have been lost in a prolonged conflict, remains a subject of intense ethical debate and scrutiny.

The miscalculations in targeting Hiroshima also included a failure to anticipate the international political and moral ramifications. The bombings of Hiroshima and, three days later, Nagasaki, where a plutonium bomb was dropped, marked the first and only use of nuclear weapons in warfare. These events highlighted the terrifying power of nuclear weapons and prompted a global reconsideration of warfare and international relations.

In the years following the bombings, Hiroshima became a symbol of the horrors of nuclear war and a focal point for anti-nuclear activism. The city's annual commemoration of the bombing serves as a reminder of the human cost of nuclear conflict and the urgent need for disarmament. The Peace Memorial Park and the Hiroshima Peace Memorial Museum educate visitors about the bombing and advocate for a world free of nuclear weapons.

The targeting of Hiroshima, driven by a combination of strategic objectives and miscalculations, had profound and lasting consequences. The devastation wrought by the atomic bomb forever altered the course of history, ushering in the nuclear age and fundamentally changing the nature of global conflict and diplomacy. The lessons learned from Hiroshima continue to resonate, emphasizing the need for careful consideration of the ethical, humanitarian, and geopolitical implications of military decisions.

Chapter 5: The BP Deepwater Horizon Blowout

The BP Deepwater Horizon blowout, which occurred on April 20, 2010, is one of the most catastrophic environmental disasters in history. This disaster resulted in the largest marine oil spill ever recorded, significantly affecting marine and coastal ecosystems, local economies, and human health. The incident was caused by a combination of mechanical failures, human errors, and organizational lapses, all of which contributed to the blowout and the subsequent environmental and economic devastation.

The Deepwater Horizon was an offshore drilling rig operated by Transocean and leased by British Petroleum (BP). The rig was located in the Macondo Prospect, about 41 miles off the coast of Louisiana, in the Gulf of Mexico. The Deepwater Horizon was drilling an exploratory well at a depth of approximately 5,000 feet below sea level and an additional 13,000 feet below the seabed. Deepwater drilling involves complex operations and high pressures, making it inherently risky and requiring meticulous planning, execution, and safety protocols.

On the evening of April 20, 2010, a series of events unfolded that led to the blowout. The crew was in the final stages of temporarily capping the Macondo well, intending to return later to extract oil. To temporarily cap the well, they used a cement seal designed to prevent hydrocarbons from flowing into the wellbore. Halliburton, a contractor, was responsible for the cementing process, while BP was overseeing the entire operation.

A crucial step in this process was the use of a spacer fluid, which is pumped down the well to separate the drilling mud from the cement. On the Deepwater Horizon, a type of spacer fluid not approved by the regulatory authorities was used. This spacer fluid did not adequately isolate the hydrocarbons, allowing gas to enter the wellbore. However, the first significant failure was the cement job itself. The cement used to seal the well was insufficiently mixed and failed to form a reliable barrier.

Despite warning signs, including unexpected pressure readings, the decision was made to proceed with displacing the drilling mud with seawater, a process that reduces the hydrostatic pressure inside the well. Displacing the drilling mud is a critical operation because drilling mud, being denser than seawater, helps keep the hydrocarbons in place. Removing the mud too early can lead to a blowout if the well is not properly sealed.

The Transocean crew conducted a series of negative pressure tests to verify the integrity of the cement seal. These tests are designed to detect leaks by reducing pressure inside the well and observing any backflow of fluids. The negative pressure tests yielded ambiguous results, but the crew misinterpreted the data, concluding that the well was secure. In reality, the cement had failed to isolate the hydrocarbons effectively, and gas was already leaking into the wellbore.

At approximately 9:45 PM, a surge of gas and drilling mud erupted onto the rig, known as a "kick." The blowout preventer (BOP), a massive piece of safety equipment designed to seal the well in an emergency, failed to activate properly. The BOP had multiple components, including a shear ram intended to cut through the drill pipe and seal the well. However, due to a combination of design flaws, maintenance issues, and operational failures, the BOP did not function as intended.

Within minutes, the gas reached the rig's deck, igniting and causing a series of explosions. The explosions engulfed the rig in flames, and the crew struggled to contain the fire and activate the emergency systems. The rig's blowout preventer control pod, which should have triggered the BOP, failed to do so due to a dead battery and a miswired solenoid valve. These technical failures rendered the BOP ineffective in sealing the well.

The situation rapidly deteriorated as the fire continued to rage, and attempts to extinguish it proved futile. The Deepwater Horizon sank on April 22, 2010, leaving the wellhead gushing oil into the Gulf of Mexico. The sinking of the rig marked the beginning of a months-long struggle to cap the well and contain the spill. Over the following 87 days, an estimated 4.9 million barrels (206 million gallons) of crude oil were released into the Gulf, making it the largest marine oil spill in history.

The environmental impact of the spill was immediate and profound. The oil spread across vast areas of the Gulf, affecting marine life, coastal ecosystems, and human communities. Beaches, marshlands, and estuaries along the Gulf Coast were heavily contaminated, leading to the death of countless marine organisms, including fish, birds, sea turtles, and dolphins. The spill disrupted the breeding and feeding grounds of many species, causing long-term ecological damage.

Efforts to cap the well involved multiple strategies and substantial technical challenges. BP deployed a series of measures, including containment domes, a "top kill" procedure (pumping heavy drilling mud into the well), and a "junk shot" (injecting debris to clog the BOP). These efforts were largely unsuccessful. It wasn't until mid-July that BP succeeded in capping the well using a containment cap, and by mid-September, a relief well was drilled to permanently seal the Macondo well.

The economic impact on the Gulf Coast was devastating. The fishing and tourism industries, vital to the region's economy, suffered severe losses. Fishing bans were imposed over vast areas, and coastal businesses faced significant declines in revenue due to contaminated waters and oil-stained beaches. The spill also led to a dramatic drop in property values and a decline in overall economic activity in affected areas.

The Deepwater Horizon disaster prompted widespread public outrage and led to extensive investigations and litigation. The U.S. government launched several inquiries, including the National Commission on the BP Deepwater Horizon Oil Spill and Offshore Drilling. The commission's final report, released in January 2011, identified multiple failures by BP, Transocean, and Halliburton, as well as systemic issues within the regulatory framework overseeing offshore drilling.

BP faced significant legal and financial repercussions. In 2012, BP agreed to a record $4.5 billion settlement with the U.S. government, which included criminal charges and penalties. Additionally, BP established a $20 billion compensation fund to address claims from affected individuals, businesses, and communities. Further civil litigation resulted in additional fines and settlements, with the total financial cost to BP exceeding $60 billion.

The disaster also prompted significant changes in offshore drilling regulations and industry practices. The U.S. government implemented stricter safety and environmental standards, including improved blowout preventer designs, enhanced well control procedures, and more rigorous inspection and oversight protocols. The industry adopted new technologies and best practices to mitigate the risks associated with deepwater drilling.

Despite these reforms, the long-term environmental and economic impacts of the Deepwater Horizon spill continue to be felt. Studies have documented persistent damage to marine and coastal ecosystems, including reduced populations of certain species, ongoing contamination of sediments, and lingering health effects on wildlife. The spill also highlighted the vulnerability of coastal communities to industrial accidents and the need for continued vigilance and preparedness in managing offshore drilling operations.

The BP Deepwater Horizon blowout serves as a stark reminder of the potential consequences of technological failures, human errors, and organizational lapses in high-risk industries. The disaster underscored the importance of robust safety cultures, effective regulatory frameworks, and continuous improvement in technology and practices to prevent similar catastrophes in the future. The legacy of the Deepwater Horizon disaster is a sobering testament to the need for balance between economic development and environmental stewardship, particularly in the pursuit of valuable but inherently risky resources like offshore oil.

Chapter 6: Apollo 13's Faulty Tank Incident

The Apollo 13 mission, famously dubbed as NASA's "successful failure," is a story of ingenuity, perseverance, and remarkable problem-solving in the face of potentially catastrophic adversity. Launched on April 11, 1970, Apollo 13 was intended to be the third manned mission to land on the Moon. However, an explosion in one of the spacecraft's oxygen tanks transformed the mission into a harrowing ordeal and a testament to the resilience and resourcefulness of the astronauts and the ground crew. The faulty tank incident not only challenged the limits of human ingenuity but also provided invaluable lessons for future space exploration.

The crew of Apollo 13 comprised three astronauts: James A. Lovell, Jr., the mission commander; John L. Swigert, Jr., the command module pilot; and Fred W. Haise, Jr., the lunar module pilot. The mission objectives included exploring the Fra Mauro highlands on the Moon, conducting scientific experiments, and deploying several scientific instruments on the lunar surface. The spacecraft consisted of two primary components: the Command/Service Module (CSM), named Odyssey, and the Lunar Module (LM), named Aquarius.

The troubles for Apollo 13 began long before the spacecraft lifted off. The origins of the faulty tank incident can be traced back to its manufacture and testing. The oxygen tank in question, designated as Tank No. 2, was part of the Service Module, which housed the main propulsion and life-support systems. During routine testing in 1968, the tank had sustained damage when it was dropped by a technician. Despite inspections and repairs, this incident set the stage for the problems that would later arise.

The tank's heating system also posed significant issues. The oxygen tanks were equipped with heaters to maintain the liquid oxygen at the necessary temperature. However, due to a miscommunication between NASA and the contractors, the voltage rating of the heaters was mismatched. The heaters were designed for 28 volts but were subjected to 65 volts during a ground test. This overheating caused the insulation on the wires inside the tank to deteriorate, creating a potential hazard that went undetected.

Apollo 13's launch proceeded smoothly, with no indication of the challenges that lay ahead. The spacecraft successfully reached Earth orbit and initiated the translunar injection burn, propelling it toward the Moon. For the first two days of the mission, operations proceeded as planned, with the crew performing routine checks and preparing for the lunar landing.

However, at approximately 55 hours and 54 minutes into the mission, disaster struck. The crew was instructed to perform a "cryo stir" to prevent the oxygen and hydrogen in the tanks from stratifying. This procedure involved activating fans within the tanks to ensure even mixing of the gases. When Swigert flipped the switch to initiate the stir, a spark ignited the damaged insulation in Oxygen Tank No. 2, causing a violent explosion. The explosion ripped through the Service Module, rupturing Oxygen Tank No. 1 and damaging vital systems.

The immediate aftermath of the explosion was chaotic and alarming. Warning lights and alarms went off in the spacecraft, and the crew quickly realized that they were losing oxygen and power. Lovell famously reported to Mission Control, "Houston, we've had a problem." The explosion had not only crippled the Service Module but also compromised the Command Module's life-support systems. The primary source of oxygen, water, and electricity for the mission was now severely impaired.

The crew and Mission Control were faced with an unprecedented crisis: how to bring the astronauts safely back to Earth with severely limited resources. The Lunar Module, designed to support two astronauts for a limited duration on the lunar surface, now had to serve as a lifeboat for all three astronauts for the journey back to Earth. This required a series of rapid and innovative problem-solving efforts by both the crew and the engineers on the ground.

One of the immediate challenges was to ensure a continued supply of oxygen and electricity. The Lunar Module had its own independent supply of oxygen, water, and batteries, but these resources were limited. The crew had to carefully ration their supplies, reducing their power consumption to a bare minimum. Non-essential systems were shut down, and the astronauts endured cold temperatures and difficult living conditions to conserve energy.

Another critical issue was the buildup of carbon dioxide. The Lunar Module's life-support system was designed for two astronauts, not three, leading to a rapid accumulation of carbon dioxide in the cabin. The onboard lithium hydroxide canisters used to scrub CO_2 were quickly being exhausted. Engineers at Mission Control devised a makeshift solution known as the "mailbox," using materials available on the spacecraft, including plastic bags, cardboard, and duct tape. This improvised device successfully allowed the Command Module's square canisters to be used in the Lunar Module's round receptacles, effectively removing CO_2 from the cabin air.

Navigational challenges also arose as a result of the explosion. The Service Module's thrusters, used for course corrections and reentry, were rendered inoperable. The Lunar Module's descent engine was repurposed to perform crucial burns to adjust the spacecraft's trajectory. These burns had to be meticulously calculated and executed to ensure that Apollo 13 remained on a free-return trajectory, allowing it to loop around the Moon and return to Earth.

One of the most nail-biting moments came during the return journey when the crew had to perform a critical burn using the Lunar Module's descent engine. With limited power and no computer assistance, the astronauts had to manually align the spacecraft using a handheld sextant and sighting on stars. The burn was executed flawlessly, placing Apollo 13 on a course for reentry into Earth's atmosphere.

As Apollo 13 approached Earth, the crew faced the final challenge of reentry. The Lunar Module was jettisoned, and the damaged Service Module was discarded, revealing the extent of the explosion's damage. The Command Module, now powered up and ready for reentry, faced the perilous journey through the atmosphere. The heat shield, designed to withstand the intense heat of reentry, held up, and the Command Module splashed down safely in the Pacific Ocean on April 17, 1970.

The recovery of the Apollo 13 crew marked the successful conclusion of a mission that could have easily ended in tragedy. The ingenuity, resilience, and teamwork displayed by the astronauts and the ground crew were nothing short of extraordinary. The mission's outcome highlighted the importance of thorough testing, rigorous safety protocols, and the ability to adapt to unforeseen circumstances.

The investigation into the Apollo 13 incident revealed the root causes of the faulty tank explosion. The damaged insulation and the mismatch in voltage ratings were identified as critical factors. The findings led to significant changes in procedures and protocols for subsequent missions, ensuring that similar failures would be prevented in the future.

Apollo 13's faulty tank incident left an indelible mark on space exploration history. It underscored the inherent risks of space travel and the need for constant vigilance and innovation. The mission became a symbol of human ingenuity and determination, demonstrating that even in the face of overwhelming odds, success is possible through collaboration and perseverance.

The lessons learned from Apollo 13 continue to influence space missions today. The meticulous planning, testing, and problem-solving approaches developed during the crisis have become integral to mission design and execution. The legacy of Apollo 13 serves as a reminder of the challenges and rewards of exploration and the unyielding human spirit that drives us to reach beyond our limits.

Chapter 7: The Gimli Glider Fuel Miscalculation

The story of the Gimli Glider, an Air Canada flight that ran out of fuel at 41,000 feet due to a miscalculation, is a remarkable tale of aviation error and ingenuity. It illustrates how a small oversight can cascade into a life-threatening situation, but also how exceptional skill and quick thinking can avert disaster. This incident, which occurred on July 23, 1983, has become a textbook case in aviation history, highlighting the importance of accurate measurements, effective communication, and the critical role of pilot training.

Flight 143, a Boeing 767, was a relatively new aircraft at the time, equipped with a sophisticated electronic flight instrument system and an innovative fuel quantity indicating system (FQIS). The aircraft was set to fly from Montreal to Edmonton, with a stopover in Ottawa. The flight crew, Captain Robert Pearson and First Officer Maurice Quintal, both experienced pilots, were responsible for ensuring the plane had sufficient fuel for the journey. However, a series of errors during the refueling process led to a critical miscalculation.

The problems began with a malfunction in the FQIS, which was supposed to provide accurate fuel quantity readings. The system had a history of intermittent faults, and on this particular day, it was completely inoperative. As a result, the flight crew had to resort to manual calculations to determine the fuel load. The process involved using dipsticks to measure the fuel in the tanks and converting these measurements to liters, kilograms, and ultimately pounds, which was the unit required by the aircraft's systems.

Compounding the issue was the recent transition by Air Canada from imperial units to metric units for fuel measurements. This change was part of a broader national move towards the metric system but had introduced a potential source of confusion in calculations. On this day, the ground crew inadvertently made a crucial error in converting the fuel quantity from liters to kilograms and then to pounds. They miscalculated the density of the fuel, leading to a significant underestimation of the amount of fuel loaded onto the aircraft.

As Flight 143 departed from Montreal and then Ottawa, there was no indication of any problem. The flight progressed normally for the first part of the journey, and the crew did not receive any warning signals from the fuel gauges, which were inoperative due to the FQIS fault. It was not until the aircraft was cruising at 41,000 feet, approximately halfway to Edmonton, that the first sign of trouble appeared. An alarm sounded in the cockpit, indicating a fuel pressure problem in one of the engines. The crew initially believed it to be a malfunctioning fuel pump and switched to the cross-feed system to use fuel from the other tank.

Shortly after, the second engine also experienced a drop in fuel pressure, and within minutes, both engines failed completely. The aircraft lost all electrical power, leaving the cockpit instruments inoperative. The pilots, faced with a sudden and unprecedented crisis, had to rely on their training and instincts to manage the situation. Captain Pearson, who had experience as a glider pilot, took control of the now-engineless plane and began gliding it towards the nearest suitable landing site.

First Officer Quintal quickly calculated that the nearest airport was too far to reach, given their altitude and the rate of descent. He then suggested an alternative: Gimli Industrial Park Airport, a former military airbase that had been converted into a motor racing track. The location was familiar to Quintal, as he had trained there during his military service. With no other viable options, Captain Pearson agreed to attempt a landing at Gimli.

The descent towards Gimli was fraught with challenges. Without engines, the aircraft lacked hydraulic power for many control surfaces and systems, making it difficult to maneuver. The pilots had to use a technique known as "ram air turbine" (RAT) deployment, which provided limited hydraulic power by using the airflow over the plane to spin a small turbine. This allowed them to control the aircraft to some extent, but it was far from ideal.

As the aircraft approached Gimli, another complication arose: the runway was being used for a local car race and was filled with people, vehicles, and obstacles. Unaware of this, the pilots continued their descent, focusing on the task of landing the glider. Captain Pearson executed a series of S-turns to reduce altitude and airspeed, a maneuver rarely performed in commercial aviation but common in glider operations. This helped to align the aircraft with the runway and manage the descent rate.

At the final stage of the approach, the pilots deployed the landing gear manually, as the normal hydraulic system was unavailable. Due to the lack of hydraulic pressure, the nose gear did not fully extend and locked into place, leaving the aircraft in a precarious nose-high attitude. Despite this, Captain Pearson managed to touch down smoothly, using the main landing gear to absorb the impact. The nose eventually settled onto the runway, and the aircraft came to a stop with minimal damage.

The landing was nothing short of miraculous, and the passengers and crew were safe. The rapid and skillful response by Captain Pearson and First Officer Quintal had averted what could have been a catastrophic crash. The aftermath of the incident involved an extensive investigation by aviation authorities to determine the root causes and prevent future occurrences. The investigation revealed the critical miscalculation during the refueling process and highlighted the need for better training and communication regarding the use of metric and imperial units.

The Gimli Glider incident led to several changes in aviation practices and procedures. One of the most significant was the reinforcement of the importance of accurate and reliable fuel quantity indicating systems. Airlines and aircraft manufacturers introduced more robust training programs for flight crews and ground personnel to ensure proper understanding and use of measurement units. Additionally, the incident underscored the necessity of effective communication and verification procedures during the refueling process to prevent similar errors.

The story of the Gimli Glider has become a legendary example of airmanship and the importance of preparedness in the face of unexpected challenges. It serves as a reminder of the potential consequences of small errors and the critical need for vigilance in all aspects of aviation operations. The incident has been studied extensively in aviation training programs and is often cited as a case study in crisis management and problem-solving under pressure.

In the years following the Gimli Glider incident, both Captain Pearson and First Officer Quintal received accolades for their exceptional handling of the emergency. Their actions demonstrated the value of rigorous training, experience, and composure in the face of adversity. The legacy of Flight 143 continues to influence aviation safety practices and serves as an enduring testament to the resilience and ingenuity of the human spirit.

Chapter 8: Mount St. Helens Eruption Underestimation

The catastrophic eruption of Mount St. Helens on May 18, 1980, stands as one of the most significant volcanic events in modern history. It resulted in widespread destruction, loss of life, and long-lasting environmental impacts. The disaster also underscored the dangers of underestimating volcanic activity and the need for better understanding and monitoring of active volcanoes. The events leading up to the eruption, the eruption itself, and its aftermath reveal the complexities of volcanic behavior and the challenges of predicting such natural disasters.

Mount St. Helens, located in southwestern Washington State, had been relatively quiet for over a century before it began to show signs of renewed activity in March 1980. The mountain is part of the Cascade Range, a volcanic arc formed by the subduction of the Juan de Fuca Plate beneath the North American Plate. This geological setting makes the region prone to volcanic activity, and Mount St. Helens was known to have erupted numerous times in the past.

The first signs of trouble appeared on March 16, 1980, when a series of small earthquakes were detected beneath the volcano. These earthquakes indicated that magma was moving beneath the surface, a potential precursor to an eruption. Over the next few weeks, the seismic activity intensified, and by the end of March, hundreds of earthquakes were occurring daily. On March 27, the volcano produced its first significant explosion in over a century, sending a plume of ash and steam into the air and creating a new crater at the summit.

Despite these warning signs, the true scale of the impending eruption was not fully understood. Volcanologists and emergency management officials were aware that Mount St. Helens was becoming increasingly active, but the potential for a catastrophic eruption was underestimated. The focus was primarily on monitoring the seismic activity and the formation of a bulge on the north flank of the volcano, which was growing at an alarming rate. This bulge indicated that magma was accumulating within the mountain, causing the north flank to swell outward.

As the weeks passed, the tension between the growing bulge and the overlying rock continued to build. Scientists recognized that this situation was precarious, but the exact nature and timing of a potential eruption remained uncertain. Public warnings were issued, and a restricted "red zone" was established around the volcano to limit access and protect lives. However, enforcing these restrictions proved challenging, and many people, including loggers, journalists, and curious onlookers, ventured into the area.

On the morning of May 18, 1980, the situation reached a critical point. At 8:32 a.m., a magnitude 5.1 earthquake struck beneath Mount St. Helens, triggering the collapse of the north flank. The bulge and the summit slid away in a massive landslide, the largest in recorded history, which in turn released the pressure on the magma chamber. This sudden release of pressure resulted in a catastrophic lateral blast that flattened forests, scorched the landscape, and propelled a cloud of hot gas and ash at speeds of up to 300 miles per hour.

The lateral blast devastated an area of approximately 230 square miles, obliterating everything in its path. Trees were snapped like matchsticks, and the blast wave traveled across ridges and valleys, leaving a stark, barren landscape in its wake. The eruption column, a towering plume of ash and gas, shot up to 80,000 feet into the atmosphere, spreading ash across multiple states and causing darkness in areas hundreds of miles away.

The immediate impact on the local environment was profound. The eruption melted snow and ice on the mountain, generating massive mudflows known as lahars. These lahars raced down river valleys, destroying bridges, homes, and infrastructure. The Toutle River, in particular, was heavily affected, with the lahars carrying vast amounts of volcanic debris downstream, clogging rivers and creating long-term flooding hazards.

The human toll of the eruption was significant. Fifty-seven people lost their lives, including scientists, photographers, and local residents who had not evacuated in time. The eruption also caused extensive economic damage, estimated at over $1 billion. Logging operations in the area were devastated, with thousands of acres of forest destroyed. The ashfall disrupted transportation, agriculture, and daily life across the Pacific Northwest.

In the aftermath of the eruption, extensive efforts were made to understand what had happened and to learn from the event. Volcanologists studied the deposits left by the eruption, mapping the distribution of ash, pumice, and other volcanic materials. These studies provided valuable insights into the dynamics of the eruption, the behavior of pyroclastic flows, and the formation of lahars. The data collected helped to refine models of volcanic activity and improve predictions for future eruptions.

One of the key lessons from the Mount St. Helens eruption was the importance of monitoring and preparedness. The eruption highlighted the need for continuous monitoring of active volcanoes, including seismic activity, ground deformation, gas emissions, and other signs of unrest. Advances in technology since 1980 have greatly enhanced the ability to monitor volcanoes in real-time, providing critical information for early warning and evacuation efforts.

The eruption also underscored the importance of public education and communication. Effective communication between scientists, emergency management officials, and the public is crucial for ensuring timely evacuations and reducing the risk to human life. The Mount St. Helens eruption led to the development of more comprehensive hazard maps, improved public outreach programs, and the establishment of protocols for responding to volcanic crises.

In the decades since the eruption, Mount St. Helens has continued to be a focal point for volcanic research and education. The area around the volcano has been designated as the Mount St. Helens National Volcanic Monument, preserving the landscape as a natural laboratory for studying volcanic processes and ecological recovery. The monument attracts scientists, educators, and tourists, providing opportunities to learn about the power and beauty of volcanic activity.

The eruption of Mount St. Helens remains a powerful reminder of the dynamic nature of our planet and the potential for sudden, dramatic changes in the environment. It serves as a case study for understanding the complexities of volcanic behavior and the challenges of predicting and responding to volcanic hazards. The lessons learned from this event continue to inform efforts to mitigate the risks associated with volcanic eruptions, helping to protect lives and property in volcanic regions around the world.

Chapter 9: The Exxon Valdez Navigational Error

The Exxon Valdez oil spill, a catastrophic environmental disaster, occurred on March 24, 1989, off the coast of Alaska. It is one of the most devastating human-caused environmental disasters in history. The incident resulted from a series of navigational errors, inadequate oversight, and systemic failures that culminated in the grounding of the oil tanker Exxon Valdez on Bligh Reef in Prince William Sound. This disaster not only spilled millions of gallons of crude oil into the pristine waters but also highlighted the profound consequences of navigational errors and the need for stringent safety and environmental regulations in the shipping industry.

The Exxon Valdez, an enormous tanker owned by the Exxon Shipping Company, was en route from the Valdez Marine Terminal in Alaska to Long Beach, California, carrying approximately 53 million gallons of crude oil. Captain Joseph Hazelwood, the vessel's master, was an experienced mariner but had a history of alcohol-related incidents. On the night of the accident, he allegedly consumed alcohol before taking command, a factor that later became a focal point of the investigation.

Prince William Sound, known for its treacherous waters and numerous navigational hazards, requires careful and precise navigation. The area is dotted with islands, reefs, and shoals, making it a challenging environment for large vessels. To mitigate the risks, the U.S. Coast Guard established a designated shipping route known as the Traffic Separation Scheme (TSS), which guides vessels safely through the sound. The TSS is intended to prevent accidents by separating inbound and outbound traffic lanes and keeping ships away from hazardous areas like Bligh Reef.

On the night of March 23, 1989, the Exxon Valdez departed the Valdez Marine Terminal under favorable weather conditions. However, soon after leaving port, Captain Hazelwood deviated from the TSS to avoid icebergs reported in the area. This deviation was a common practice for tankers, but it required precise navigation to ensure a safe return to the designated shipping lanes. Captain Hazelwood, trusting his experience and the ship's advanced navigational equipment, handed over control to Third Mate Gregory Cousins and retired to his quarters.

Third Mate Cousins, an experienced officer but relatively new to the Exxon Valdez, was tasked with navigating the vessel back into the TSS. Accompanied by an able seaman acting as the helmsman, Cousins relied on radar, charts, and visual aids to guide the ship. However, a critical error occurred: Cousins failed to make a crucial turn back into the shipping lanes at a key waypoint, known as the Bligh Reef buoy. This oversight set the vessel on a collision course with Bligh Reef.

Several factors contributed to this navigational error. Firstly, the ship's radar, which was capable of detecting the reef, was not functioning correctly. Although the radar issue was known, it had not been repaired, leaving the crew without a crucial tool for detecting hazards. Secondly, the able seaman at the helm, inexperienced and unfamiliar with the vessel's controls, struggled to maintain the ship's course. This lack of proficiency in critical situations further compounded the problem.

Additionally, communication breakdowns played a significant role in the disaster. Captain Hazelwood, despite being the master of the vessel, did not remain on the bridge to supervise the critical navigation through the treacherous waters. His absence, coupled with a lack of clear instructions and oversight, left Third Mate Cousins and the helmsman to navigate without adequate support. This lapse in communication and leadership was a critical factor in the failure to correct the vessel's course in time.

As the Exxon Valdez approached Bligh Reef, the gravity of the situation became apparent. Third Mate Cousins, realizing the impending collision, attempted to take evasive action by ordering a turn to starboard. However, it was too late. At approximately 12:04 AM on March 24, 1989, the Exxon Valdez struck Bligh Reef, tearing open the hull and causing crude oil to spill into the pristine waters of Prince William Sound. The immediate aftermath was chaotic as the crew tried to assess the damage and contain the spill, but the scale of the disaster quickly overwhelmed their efforts.

The consequences of the spill were catastrophic. Approximately 11 million gallons of crude oil spilled into the sound, creating a massive oil slick that spread over 1,300 miles of coastline. The spill had a devastating impact on the region's fragile ecosystem, affecting a wide range of marine life, including fish, seabirds, sea otters, and whales. The oil contaminated critical habitats, such as spawning grounds for salmon and herring, and the resulting damage to these species had cascading effects on the entire food web.

The cleanup efforts were extensive but challenging. Exxon Mobil Corporation, the parent company of Exxon Shipping, mobilized resources to contain and remove the oil. Thousands of workers, including local fishermen and volunteers, participated in the cleanup operations, using booms, skimmers, and chemical dispersants to combat the spill. Despite these efforts, the remote and rugged terrain of Prince William Sound made the cleanup process slow and difficult. Large quantities of oil remained trapped in inaccessible areas, where it continued to cause long-term environmental damage.

The Exxon Valdez spill also had profound social and economic impacts on the local communities. The commercial fishing industry, a vital source of livelihood for many Alaskan residents, was devastated by the contamination of fish stocks and the disruption of fishing activities. The tourism industry also suffered, as the spill marred the region's natural beauty and deterred visitors. The disaster led to widespread outrage and legal battles, with affected communities seeking compensation for their losses.

In the wake of the spill, a comprehensive investigation was launched to determine the causes and hold those responsible accountable. The National Transportation Safety Board (NTSB) conducted an in-depth analysis of the events leading up to the accident. The investigation revealed a series of systemic failures, including inadequate training and oversight, lax safety protocols, and the failure to repair critical equipment like the radar. Captain Hazelwood faced criminal charges, including operating a vessel while intoxicated, but was ultimately acquitted of the most serious charges. However, he was found guilty of a lesser charge of negligent discharge of oil and was fined and ordered to perform community service.

The Exxon Valdez disaster prompted significant changes in the regulation and oversight of the shipping industry. The Oil Pollution Act of 1990 (OPA 90) was enacted in response to the spill, establishing stricter safety and environmental standards for oil tankers and improving the nation's ability to respond to oil spills. OPA 90 mandated double-hull designs for new tankers, increased liability limits for oil spills, and required the development of contingency plans for spill response. The act also created the Oil Spill Liability Trust Fund, which provides financial resources for cleanup and compensation in the event of future spills.

The Exxon Valdez spill also led to improvements in navigational practices and technology. The importance of reliable radar and other navigational aids was underscored, leading to stricter maintenance and inspection protocols. Training programs for crew members were enhanced to ensure they were adequately prepared to handle critical navigation and emergency situations. The incident also emphasized the need for better communication and leadership on the bridge, reinforcing the principle that the master of the vessel must remain actively engaged in navigating hazardous waters.

The legacy of the Exxon Valdez spill continues to influence environmental policy and practices. The disaster raised public awareness about the risks associated with oil transportation and the need for robust safeguards to protect marine environments. It also highlighted the importance of holding corporations accountable for environmental damage and ensuring that they take proactive measures to prevent such incidents. The spill remains a stark reminder of the devastating impact that human error and systemic failures can have on the environment and communities.

Chapter 10: The Bhopal Gas Leak Negligence

The Bhopal gas leak is one of the most catastrophic industrial disasters in history, resulting from a series of negligent actions and oversights. It occurred on the night of December 2-3, 1984, at the Union Carbide India Limited (UCIL) pesticide plant in Bhopal, Madhya Pradesh, India. The disaster unfolded when a storage tank containing methyl isocyanate (MIC), a highly toxic chemical, began to leak. The consequences of this leak were devastating, leading to immediate and long-term health effects on the population of Bhopal.

Union Carbide Corporation (UCC), an American company, established the plant in Bhopal in 1969 through its subsidiary UCIL. The plant was built to produce Sevin, a pesticide, with MIC being one of the key ingredients. From the onset, there were issues with the plant's design, maintenance, and safety protocols. Cost-cutting measures led to substandard safety practices and equipment. For instance, the refrigeration system meant to keep the MIC at a low temperature to prevent chemical reactions had been turned off to save costs. Additionally, the gas scrubber, which could neutralize escaping gases, was not functional, and the flare tower, designed to burn off gases, was also inoperative at the time of the leak.

On the fateful night, water entered Tank 610, which contained over 40 tons of MIC. This triggered a runaway exothermic reaction, causing the temperature and pressure inside the tank to rise rapidly. The emergency relief valve opened, releasing a large volume of toxic gas into the atmosphere. The gas, being heavier than air, spread quickly over the densely populated shantytowns around the plant. People woke up coughing, their eyes burning, and many succumbed to the effects of the gas as they tried to flee. The MIC, along with other gases released, caused immediate deaths due to respiratory failure, choking, and pulmonary edema. Those who survived the initial exposure suffered long-term health issues, including blindness, organ damage, and genetic defects.

The immediate aftermath of the disaster was chaotic. Hospitals were overwhelmed with thousands of patients, and there was a lack of adequate medical treatment for MIC exposure. The local government and Union Carbide's response were criticized as inadequate and delayed. UCC's chairman, Warren Anderson, was arrested when he visited Bhopal but was released on bail and left India, never to return for trial despite multiple summonses. The legal and compensation battle that followed was protracted and contentious. In 1989, Union Carbide settled with the Indian government for $470 million, a sum widely criticized as insufficient given the scale of the disaster. Victims and their families felt that justice had not been served, and the funds were inadequate to cover medical expenses and rehabilitation.

The site of the UCIL plant remained contaminated for years, with toxic chemicals seeping into the ground and water, causing ongoing health issues for the local population. Efforts to clean up the site were slow and insufficient. The disaster highlighted severe deficiencies in industrial safety standards and regulatory oversight. It exposed the dangers of multinational companies operating in developing countries with lax enforcement of safety protocols and environmental regulations. The Bhopal gas leak also led to changes in industrial safety legislation and practices worldwide. In India, it prompted the introduction of stricter regulations for hazardous industries and improved emergency response mechanisms. Internationally, it underscored the need for corporate accountability and better safety standards to prevent such disasters.

The long-term impact on the survivors has been profound. Many have suffered chronic health problems, including respiratory issues, cancers, and neurological disorders. Children born to affected parents often have congenital disabilities and developmental problems. The psychological trauma of the disaster, compounded by inadequate compensation and ongoing health struggles, has left deep scars on the community. Activists and survivors have continued to fight for justice, better compensation, and proper medical care. Their efforts have kept the memory of the disaster alive and highlighted the need for continued vigilance and improvement in industrial safety standards.

The Bhopal disaster is a grim reminder of the catastrophic potential of industrial negligence. It emphasizes the importance of stringent safety protocols, proper maintenance of safety equipment, and the need for comprehensive emergency response plans. It also calls attention to the ethical responsibility of corporations to ensure the safety and well-being of the communities in which they operate. The legacy of Bhopal serves as a cautionary tale, urging constant vigilance and commitment to safety in industrial operations worldwide.

This disaster underscores the critical need for robust legal frameworks to hold corporations accountable and ensure they adhere to safety standards. The failure of the legal system to provide adequate justice and compensation for the victims remains a contentious issue. The international community must learn from Bhopal and work towards preventing similar tragedies in the future. This includes fostering a culture of safety, transparency, and accountability in industries handling hazardous materials. The story of Bhopal is not just a narrative of a single night of horror but a long-lasting tragedy with lessons that must inform future industrial practices and policies.

The continued suffering of Bhopal's survivors and the environmental damage serves as a stark reminder of the consequences of neglect and the need for rigorous safety measures. The disaster also highlights the disparity in how industrial accidents are managed and compensated in different parts of the world. The Bhopal gas leak remains a poignant example of how minor errors, when compounded by negligence and cost-cutting measures, can lead to major, devastating consequences. It is a call to action for industry leaders, policymakers, and regulators to prioritize human lives and the environment over profits and to ensure that such a tragedy never happens again.

44

Chapter 11: The Tacoma Narrows Bridge Collapse

The Tacoma Narrows Bridge collapse, often referred to as "Galloping Gertie," stands as one of the most famous engineering failures in history, serving as a dramatic illustration of the consequences of insufficient understanding of aerodynamic forces in bridge design. Opened to traffic on July 1, 1940, the Tacoma Narrows Bridge was the third-longest suspension bridge in the world at the time, spanning the Puget Sound between Tacoma and the Kitsap Peninsula in Washington State. However, its collapse just four months later, on November 7, 1940, has left a lasting impact on the fields of civil engineering and bridge design.

The design of the Tacoma Narrows Bridge was ambitious, with a main span of 2,800 feet (850 meters). Its sleek, narrow profile, intended to reduce material costs and aesthetic impact, ultimately contributed to its vulnerability. The bridge's relatively shallow and narrow roadbed, with a width of just 39 feet (12 meters) and a depth of only 8 feet (2.4 meters), made it susceptible to oscillations and aerodynamic forces. Leon Moisseiff, the designer of the bridge, applied then-modern theories of deflection, but the aerodynamics of such long, slender structures were not fully understood at the time.

From its opening day, the bridge exhibited unusual behavior, earning the nickname "Galloping Gertie" due to its tendency to undulate in the wind. These oscillations, while concerning, were initially thought to be harmless. Engineers and motorists observed the bridge's movements with curiosity rather than alarm. The vertical oscillations, caused by aerodynamic flutter, were a result of the interaction between the bridge's structure and the wind. The bridge would rise and fall, creating waves that traveled along its length.

Despite these noticeable movements, the bridge was deemed safe for use.

The pivotal moment came on the morning of November 7, 1940. A steady wind of around 42 miles per hour (68 kilometers per hour) blew through the Tacoma Narrows. This wind speed, while not exceptionally high, was sufficient to set off a catastrophic sequence of events. The bridge entered into a state of torsional oscillation, where the deck began to twist along its longitudinal axis. This torsional motion was fundamentally different from the vertical oscillations previously observed. The bridge's centerline twisted in one direction while the edges moved in the opposite direction, creating a twisting wave that propagated along the span.

This torsional motion grew in amplitude, reaching a point where the bridge's movements became extreme. The oscillations were so severe that the roadway twisted more than 45 degrees from horizontal. The bridge's materials, stressed beyond their limits, began to fail. Suspender cables snapped, and sections of the deck broke loose and fell into the water below. Remarkably, the only casualty of the collapse was a dog trapped in a car abandoned by its owner. This fortunate outcome was due in part to the fact that the bridge's movements made it difficult for vehicles to stay on the road, prompting most drivers to abandon their cars and flee to safety.

The collapse of the Tacoma Narrows Bridge was captured on film, providing a stark visual record of the event. The footage shows the bridge twisting violently, parts of the deck breaking away, and finally, the entire structure collapsing into the Puget Sound. This dramatic imagery has been studied extensively by engineers and remains a powerful reminder of the importance of understanding aerodynamic forces in bridge design.

In the aftermath of the collapse, an extensive investigation was conducted to determine the causes and to prevent future occurrences. The principal cause was identified as aeroelastic flutter, a phenomenon where aerodynamic forces interact with a structure's natural frequencies, causing oscillations to increase in amplitude until failure occurs. The bridge's narrow design, coupled with its relatively light weight and lack of sufficient damping mechanisms, made it particularly susceptible to this effect. Additionally, the solid plate girder design used for the deck allowed wind to create lift forces that exacerbated the oscillations.

The lessons learned from the Tacoma Narrows Bridge collapse led to significant advancements in the field of bridge engineering. The incident underscored the need for rigorous wind tunnel testing and aerodynamic analysis in the design of long-span suspension bridges. Engineers recognized the importance of incorporating aerodynamic stability into bridge designs, leading to innovations such as open trusses, perforated decks, and the addition of dampers to dissipate energy from oscillations. These measures help to mitigate the effects of wind and reduce the risk of aeroelastic flutter.

The collapse also highlighted the importance of interdisciplinary collaboration in engineering projects. The integration of aerodynamicists, structural engineers, and material scientists became essential in the design of large-scale structures. This holistic approach ensures that all potential forces and interactions are considered, leading to safer and more resilient designs. Moreover, the Tacoma Narrows Bridge collapse emphasized the value of continuous monitoring and maintenance of infrastructure. Modern bridges are equipped with sensors and monitoring systems that provide real-time data on structural behavior, allowing for early detection of potential issues and timely interventions.

The replacement bridge, which opened in 1950, incorporated many of the lessons learned from the original bridge's failure. Designed with a deeper and stiffer deck and open trusses to allow wind to pass through, the new Tacoma Narrows Bridge has stood the test of time without experiencing the same issues as its predecessor. This new design, coupled with advancements in materials and construction techniques, has provided a safer and more reliable crossing for the region.

The legacy of the Tacoma Narrows Bridge collapse extends beyond the field of civil engineering. It serves as a case study in engineering ethics, highlighting the responsibility of engineers to anticipate and mitigate potential risks. The disaster also underscores the importance of public safety and the need for transparent communication between engineers, government officials, and the public. Ensuring that safety concerns are addressed and that the community is informed about potential risks is crucial in maintaining public trust in engineering projects.

The Tacoma Narrows Bridge collapse remains a powerful example of the consequences of overlooking complex interactions between structural elements and environmental forces. It serves as a reminder that engineering is an evolving discipline, requiring constant learning and adaptation. The disaster prompted a reevaluation of engineering principles and practices, leading to more robust and resilient infrastructure designs worldwide. The lessons learned from Galloping Gertie continue to inform the design and construction of bridges, contributing to the safety and reliability of transportation networks globally.

Chapter 12: The Great Chicago Fire Lantern Accident

The Great Chicago Fire of 1871 stands as one of the most infamous urban conflagrations in American history. Its origins are shrouded in legend and speculation, with the most popular story attributing the cause to a cow kicking over a lantern in the barn of Mrs. Catherine O'Leary. Whether this tale is fact or fiction, the fire's impact on Chicago and its subsequent rebuilding efforts were profound and far-reaching.

The fire began on the evening of October 8, 1871, in a small barn belonging to Patrick and Catherine O'Leary on DeKoven Street. The city of Chicago at the time was a tinderbox waiting to ignite. A combination of factors made the city particularly vulnerable to fire. First, an extended period of drought had left the wooden buildings, streets, and sidewalks extremely dry. Second, most structures in Chicago were made of wood, including houses, businesses, and even sidewalks. Many buildings were topped with highly flammable tar or shingle roofs, and the construction density in the city meant that fire could easily spread from one building to another.

The exact cause of the fire remains a subject of debate. While the story of Mrs. O'Leary's cow has captured the public imagination, it is likely an apocryphal tale. An investigative reporter named Michael Ahern admitted in 1893 that he had fabricated the story for a newspaper article. Despite this, the legend persisted, and Mrs. O'Leary and her cow became scapegoats for the disaster. Other theories about the fire's origin include the possibility of humans accidentally starting it, whether through a stray spark from a chimney or a careless smoker. Regardless of its true cause, the fire rapidly grew out of control.

The Chicago Fire Department, already exhausted from fighting multiple smaller fires in the days leading up to the Great Fire, was ill-prepared for the massive inferno. The initial alarm was sounded at 9:40 p.m., but a series of miscommunications and errors delayed the response. By the time firefighters arrived at the O'Leary barn, the fire had spread to neighboring buildings. Strong winds from the southwest fanned the flames, propelling them through the densely packed wooden structures. The fire quickly engulfed blocks, leaping from rooftop to rooftop and spreading through the wooden sidewalks.

As the firestorm grew, it created its own weather system, with intense heat causing superheated air to rise rapidly, drawing in cooler air at ground level. This phenomenon, known as a fire whirl or fire tornado, further spread the flames. The firestorm raged throughout the night and into the next day. Efforts to contain it were hampered by a lack of water pressure, as the city's waterworks were destroyed early in the blaze. Firefighters were forced to retreat repeatedly as the fire advanced, unable to gain any ground against the inferno.

By the time the fire was finally brought under control on October 10, it had consumed approximately 3.3 square miles (9 square kilometers) of the city. The devastation was immense: around 17,500 buildings were destroyed, leaving over 100,000 people—about a third of the city's population—homeless. The fire caused an estimated $200 million in damages, a staggering sum at the time. Miraculously, the official death toll was relatively low, with estimates ranging from 300 to 500, although the exact number is unknown and may be higher, as many bodies were likely incinerated or went unreported.

The aftermath of the Great Chicago Fire saw a massive outpouring of aid from across the country and around the world. Donations of money, food, clothing, and other supplies poured into Chicago to help the displaced residents. Temporary shelters were established, and efforts to provide food and medical care to the victims were quickly organized. Despite the devastation, the people of Chicago demonstrated remarkable resilience and determination in the face of disaster.

The city embarked on an ambitious and rapid rebuilding effort. Within days, plans were being drawn up to reconstruct Chicago, with a focus on creating a more fire-resistant urban landscape. Building codes were revised to mandate the use of fireproof materials such as brick, stone, and iron in new construction. The wooden sidewalks were replaced with stone and concrete, and firebreaks were incorporated into the city's design to prevent future fires from spreading so easily. The rebuilding effort attracted architects, engineers, and laborers from across the country, transforming Chicago into a hub of innovation and modern urban planning.

One of the most significant outcomes of the fire was the rise of the Chicago School of Architecture, which pioneered the use of steel-frame construction in high-rise buildings. This innovation allowed for the creation of taller and more durable structures, fundamentally changing the skyline of Chicago and influencing urban architecture worldwide. Notable architects such as Daniel Burnham and Louis Sullivan emerged during this period, contributing to the development of modern skyscrapers.

The Great Chicago Fire also had a profound impact on the field of fire safety and prevention. The disaster underscored the importance of having effective fire-fighting infrastructure and protocols in place. Cities across the United States and beyond began to implement stricter building codes, improve fire-fighting equipment and training, and develop comprehensive fire response plans. The fire highlighted the need for better urban planning and zoning laws to prevent the kind of unchecked growth and dense construction that had made Chicago so vulnerable.

In the years following the fire, Chicago experienced a remarkable economic and cultural resurgence. The city's strategic location as a transportation hub, combined with its resilient population and influx of investment, helped it to quickly rebuild and grow. By the end of the 19th century, Chicago had become one of the largest and most important cities in the United States, known for its booming industries, vibrant cultural scene, and architectural innovation.

The Great Chicago Fire remains a pivotal event in the city's history, remembered both for the immense destruction it caused and for the remarkable recovery and growth that followed. The legacy of the fire is evident in Chicago's modern skyline, its architectural heritage, and its status as a major global city. The story of the fire and the subsequent rebuilding serves as a powerful testament to human resilience, ingenuity, and the ability to turn tragedy into an opportunity for renewal and progress.

Chapter 13: The 1977 Tenerife Airport Collision

The 1977 Tenerife airport collision remains one of the deadliest aviation disasters in history, resulting from a complex series of miscommunications, errors, and unfortunate circumstances. The collision involved two Boeing 747 jumbo jets on the runway of Los Rodeos Airport (now Tenerife North Airport) on the Spanish Canary Island of Tenerife. On March 27, 1977, a KLM Royal Dutch Airlines Boeing 747, operating as Flight 4805, collided with a Pan American World Airways Boeing 747, Flight 1736, in dense fog, killing 583 of the 644 people on board both aircraft.

The disaster was set in motion by a terrorist incident at Gran Canaria Airport, the intended destination for both flights. A bomb explosion at Gran Canaria, located on a neighboring island, led to the temporary closure of the airport. As a result, many incoming flights, including the KLM and Pan Am 747s, were diverted to Los Rodeos Airport, a smaller airport not equipped to handle such an influx of large aircraft. The congestion at Los Rodeos contributed to the chaotic environment on the ground.

Los Rodeos Airport had a single main runway with a parallel taxiway. Due to the sudden surge in traffic, the taxiway became overcrowded, forcing aircraft to taxi on the runway itself. The KLM 747, piloted by Captain Jacob Veldhuyzen van Zanten, and the Pan Am 747, piloted by Captain Victor Grubbs, were among the planes waiting to depart once Gran Canaria reopened. The dense fog that enveloped the airport later in the day reduced visibility to less than 1,000 feet (300 meters), exacerbating the challenges faced by the air traffic controllers and the pilots.

Communication issues played a crucial role in the disaster. The air traffic control tower at Los Rodeos was using a single frequency to communicate with all the aircraft, leading to radio congestion and occasional interference. Non-standard phraseology and language barriers further complicated the situation. The controllers, who were Spanish, communicated in English, the international aviation language, but occasional lapses into Spanish added to the confusion.

At around 5:00 PM, Gran Canaria Airport reopened, and both the KLM and Pan Am flights were cleared to return. The KLM aircraft was instructed to taxi down the entire length of the runway and then make a 180-degree turn to prepare for takeoff. The Pan Am aircraft was instructed to follow the KLM down the runway and then exit onto the third taxiway to clear the runway for the KLM's departure. However, in the dense fog, the Pan Am crew missed the first two taxiway exits and was still on the runway when the KLM plane reached its takeoff position.

A critical miscommunication occurred as the KLM aircraft prepared for departure. Believing that they had been cleared for takeoff, Captain Van Zanten advanced the throttles and began the takeoff roll without explicit clearance from the tower. At the same time, the Pan Am aircraft was still taxiing down the runway. When the Pan Am crew reported that they were still on the runway, the KLM flight engineer expressed his concern to Captain Van Zanten, but the captain dismissed it, convinced that they had been cleared for takeoff.

The Pan Am crew, upon realizing the KLM aircraft was accelerating towards them, attempted to communicate their position on the runway. However, their transmissions were overridden by the simultaneous radio calls from the KLM aircraft. The air traffic controller, realizing the imminent danger, tried to warn both aircraft, but it was too late. The KLM 747, traveling at over 160 mph (260 km/ h), collided with the Pan Am aircraft as it attempted to take off.

The impact sheared off the top of the Pan Am aircraft, igniting a massive fireball. The KLM aircraft became airborne briefly before crashing back onto the runway and sliding into a fiery wreck. All 248 passengers and crew aboard the KLM flight were killed. On the Pan Am flight, 335 passengers and crew perished, but remarkably, 61 people survived, primarily those seated in the forward section of the aircraft.

The aftermath of the Tenerife disaster led to widespread changes in aviation safety protocols, communication procedures, and pilot training. One of the key lessons learned was the importance of standard phraseology in aviation communications. The International Civil Aviation Organization (ICAO) implemented stricter regulations to ensure clear and unambiguous communication between pilots and air traffic controllers. Phrases such as "takeoff" and "departure" were standardized to prevent misunderstandings. For example, the term "takeoff" is now only used when actually clearing an aircraft for takeoff, replacing earlier practices where the term was used more loosely.

The disaster also highlighted the critical role of cockpit resource management (CRM), which emphasizes effective communication, teamwork, and decision-making among flight crew members. CRM training became mandatory for commercial pilots worldwide, ensuring that all crew members feel empowered to speak up and challenge decisions that may compromise safety. The concept of a "sterile cockpit" was also reinforced, requiring that non-essential conversations and activities be minimized during critical phases of flight, such as taxi, takeoff, and landing.

Technological advancements also emerged in response to the Tenerife collision. Ground radar systems were upgraded and installed at more airports to provide air traffic controllers with better situational awareness, especially in low-visibility conditions. Additionally, the development and implementation of the Traffic Collision Avoidance System (TCAS) provided an additional layer of safety by allowing aircraft to independently monitor and avoid potential mid-air collisions through automated alerts and commands to pilots.

The Tenerife disaster also led to improvements in airport infrastructure and design. Runway and taxiway markings, lighting systems, and signage were enhanced to ensure better visibility and navigation for pilots. Airports began incorporating more parallel taxiways and additional runways to reduce the need for aircraft to backtrack on active runways. Emergency response procedures were also refined, ensuring that rescue and firefighting teams could quickly and effectively respond to aviation accidents.

The cultural impact of the Tenerife disaster extended beyond the aviation industry. The tragedy underscored the importance of global cooperation in improving aviation safety standards. International aviation authorities, airlines, and pilots' unions worked together to share knowledge and implement best practices, fostering a culture of safety that continues to evolve and improve. The disaster also brought attention to the human factors that contribute to accidents, leading to ongoing research and development in the field of human performance and behavior in aviation.

In the years following the Tenerife collision, memorials and commemorations have honored the victims and survivors of the disaster. These memorials serve as a reminder of the lives lost and the lessons learned, reinforcing the aviation community's commitment to preventing similar tragedies in the future. The legacy of the Tenerife disaster is one of resilience and progress, with each advancement in aviation safety representing a step towards ensuring that the skies remain safe for all who travel.

Chapter 14: The Therac-25 Radiation Overdose

The Therac-25 radiation overdose incidents of the 1980s represent a harrowing chapter in the history of medical technology, underscoring the critical importance of rigorous software testing, system safety, and human factors engineering. The Therac-25 was a computer-controlled radiation therapy machine developed by Atomic Energy of Canada Limited (AECL) and CGR in France. It was an advanced model of its predecessors, the Therac-6 and Therac-20, designed to treat cancer patients with high-energy radiation. Unfortunately, design flaws and software errors in the Therac-25 led to at least six known cases of severe radiation overdoses between 1985 and 1987, resulting in serious injuries and deaths.

The Therac-25 incidents occurred primarily due to a combination of hardware and software failures, compounded by inadequate testing and poor user interface design. Unlike its predecessors, the Therac-25 relied heavily on software controls to manage the complex tasks of delivering precise radiation doses. This reliance on software introduced a new layer of risk, as errors in programming could directly affect the machine's operation. AECL believed that the extensive software testing conducted on the Therac-20 was sufficient to ensure the Therac-25's safety, an assumption that proved tragically incorrect.

The Therac-25 offered two modes of operation: electron mode and photon mode. Electron mode used a low-energy electron beam for surface tumors, while photon mode used a high-energy x-ray beam for deeper tumors. The machine's electron beam was designed to be highly concentrated, and in photon mode, a tungsten target was placed in the beam's path to convert electrons into x-rays. This process required precise coordination to avoid delivering excessive radiation doses. Unfortunately, the software controlling these transitions was flawed.

One critical issue was the race condition in the software, a type of error where the timing of certain operations could cause unpredictable behavior. The Therac-25's software had a race condition involving the positioning of the tungsten target and the activation of the electron beam. If an operator rapidly entered commands, the software could skip safety checks, allowing the machine to deliver a high-energy electron beam without the tungsten target in place. This resulted in a massive overdose of radiation to patients.

The user interface of the Therac-25 also contributed to the problem. The machine's operators were provided with minimal feedback regarding the machine's status and error messages were often cryptic and uninformative. For example, the machine might display an error code without explaining the nature or severity of the problem, leading operators to reset the system and resume treatment without understanding the underlying issue. This lack of clear communication and guidance significantly increased the risk of operator error.

One of the first known incidents occurred in Marietta, Georgia, in June 1985. A patient received a massive overdose of radiation, resulting in severe burns and eventual death. The incident was initially attributed to operator error, and AECL made minimal changes to the machine's design or software. Over the next two years, several more incidents occurred, each resulting in serious injuries or fatalities. In 1986, a patient in Tyler, Texas, received an overdose that caused extensive tissue damage and led to her death. Another incident in Yakima, Washington, in 1987 left a patient permanently disabled.

Investigations into these incidents revealed the extent of the Therac-25's design flaws. It became apparent that the software had not been adequately tested for safety-critical failures, and the reliance on software to control safety mechanisms introduced significant vulnerabilities. Additionally, AECL's response to initial reports of problems was slow and inadequate. The company's engineers initially denied the possibility of software errors, focusing instead on blaming operator error or hardware malfunctions.

The Food and Drug Administration (FDA) and the Canadian Radiation Protection Bureau (CRPB) eventually intervened, conducting thorough investigations and issuing safety alerts. AECL was required to implement several modifications to the Therac-25, including hardware interlocks to ensure that the tungsten target was in place before the electron beam could be activated. They also improved the software to eliminate race conditions and added more comprehensive error messages to assist operators in diagnosing problems.

The Therac-25 incidents had far-reaching implications for the field of medical device safety and regulation. They highlighted the need for rigorous software validation and verification processes, especially in systems where software errors could have life-threatening consequences. The incidents also underscored the importance of user-centered design, ensuring that operators are provided with clear and actionable information to prevent errors.

In response to the Therac-25 disasters, regulatory bodies such as the FDA introduced stricter guidelines for the development and testing of medical devices. These guidelines emphasized the importance of risk management, requiring manufacturers to identify potential hazards and implement safeguards to mitigate them. The concept of "fail-safe" design became a key principle, ensuring that even if a system fails, it does so in a way that minimizes harm to patients.

The field of human factors engineering also gained prominence as a result of the Therac-25 incidents. Human factors engineering focuses on designing systems that take into account human capabilities and limitations, aiming to reduce the likelihood of human error. This discipline emphasizes the importance of intuitive user interfaces, clear communication, and comprehensive training for operators. By addressing the interaction between humans and machines, human factors engineering seeks to create safer and more reliable systems.

The legacy of the Therac-25 is evident in the ongoing evolution of safety standards and practices in the medical device industry. Today, medical devices undergo extensive testing and validation to ensure their safety and efficacy. Regulatory bodies continue to refine their guidelines to keep pace with technological advancements, and manufacturers are held to high standards of accountability. The lessons learned from the Therac-25 have contributed to a culture of safety and continuous improvement, with the goal of preventing similar tragedies in the future.

In addition to regulatory changes, the Therac-25 incidents have had a lasting impact on the education and training of engineers and software developers. Case studies of the Therac-25 are often included in engineering curricula to illustrate the importance of safety-critical system design. These case studies serve as a sobering reminder of the potential consequences of design flaws and the ethical responsibility of engineers to prioritize safety in their work.

The Therac-25 incidents also underscored the importance of effective communication and collaboration among stakeholders. In the aftermath of the disasters, medical professionals, engineers, regulators, and manufacturers recognized the need for open and transparent communication to identify and address safety concerns. Collaborative efforts to share knowledge and best practices have contributed to the development of safer medical technologies and improved patient outcomes.

The victims of the Therac-25 radiation overdoses and their families have played a crucial role in raising awareness of the need for stringent safety measures in medical devices. Their experiences and advocacy have inspired efforts to improve patient safety and prevent future tragedies. Memorials and tributes to the victims serve as a reminder of the human cost of engineering failures and the importance of learning from past mistakes.

61

Chapter 15: The Mars Climate Orbiter Conversion Error

The Mars Climate Orbiter (MCO) conversion error of 1999 is a notorious example of how a seemingly minor oversight can lead to the failure of a major space mission. This incident involved a critical miscalculation stemming from a unit conversion error, which ultimately caused the spacecraft to deviate from its intended trajectory and disintegrate upon entering the Martian atmosphere. This failure highlights the importance of meticulous attention to detail, rigorous verification processes, and effective communication within complex engineering projects.

The Mars Climate Orbiter was part of NASA's Mars Surveyor '98 program, which also included the Mars Polar Lander. The MCO was designed to study Mars' atmosphere, climate, and surface weather conditions. Its primary objectives included mapping the distribution of water vapor, measuring atmospheric temperatures, and capturing high-resolution images of the Martian surface. The mission aimed to enhance our understanding of Martian weather patterns and climate variations, contributing valuable data for future manned missions to Mars.

The spacecraft was launched on December 11, 1998, aboard a Delta II rocket from Cape Canaveral Air Force Station. After a successful launch and an initial journey of about 416 million miles (670 million kilometers), the MCO was scheduled to enter orbit around Mars on September 23, 1999. The mission proceeded smoothly during the cruise phase, with the spacecraft making several trajectory correction maneuvers (TCMs) to ensure it stayed on the proper course to Mars.

However, as the spacecraft approached Mars, the navigation team at NASA's Jet Propulsion Laboratory (JPL) noticed a discrepancy between the expected and actual trajectory data. The deviation was minor but significant enough to raise concerns. Despite attempts to correct the trajectory, the error persisted, leading to the catastrophic failure of the mission.

The root cause of the failure was traced back to a unit conversion error. The spacecraft's navigation system, which was developed by Lockheed Martin Astronautics, utilized imperial units (pound-force seconds) for measuring force, while NASA's navigation team used metric units (newton-seconds). Specifically, the software responsible for generating the spacecraft's thrust data produced outputs in pound-force seconds, but these values were incorrectly interpreted as newton-seconds by the navigation team at JPL. This discrepancy resulted in the calculation of incorrect thrust values, leading to erroneous trajectory corrections.

To understand the gravity of this error, it is essential to grasp the magnitude of the miscalculation. One pound-force second is equivalent to approximately 4.45 newton-seconds. The failure to convert these units correctly meant that the spacecraft's propulsion system was exerting only about 22% of the necessary force required to maintain the intended trajectory. This underestimation of thrust caused the MCO to gradually drift off course over the course of its journey to Mars.

During the critical orbital insertion maneuver, which was intended to place the spacecraft into a stable orbit around Mars, the trajectory deviation proved disastrous. Instead of entering a near-circular orbit as planned, the spacecraft dipped too low into the Martian atmosphere. The excessive atmospheric drag generated intense aerodynamic forces and heat, leading to the destruction of the Mars Climate Orbiter. The spacecraft, valued at $327.6 million, was lost, along with its scientific instruments and the data they were meant to collect.

The failure of the Mars Climate Orbiter prompted a thorough investigation by NASA. The investigation revealed several contributing factors beyond the unit conversion error itself. One key issue was the lack of robust verification and validation processes. The discrepancy between the units used by Lockheed Martin and JPL should have been identified and corrected during the integration and testing phases of the project. However, insufficient checks and cross-verifications allowed the error to persist unnoticed.

Another contributing factor was the communication gap between the different teams involved in the mission. Effective communication and collaboration are vital in complex engineering projects, especially those involving multiple organizations and disciplines. In the case of the Mars Climate Orbiter, there was a breakdown in communication between the engineering teams at Lockheed Martin and the navigation team at JPL. This lack of clear communication and coordination prevented the early detection and correction of the unit conversion error.

The investigation also highlighted the importance of maintaining strict adherence to established protocols and procedures. NASA had rigorous standards and guidelines for spacecraft design, testing, and operations. However, in the case of the Mars Climate Orbiter, there were deviations from these standards. For instance, the use of imperial units in the software provided by Lockheed Martin was not consistent with NASA's preference for metric units, leading to the critical error.

In response to the failure, NASA implemented several changes to prevent similar incidents in future missions. One of the key measures was the reinforcement of stringent verification and validation processes. This included rigorous cross-checking of all units and calculations used in spacecraft design and navigation. Additionally, NASA emphasized the importance of thorough documentation and clear communication between all parties involved in a mission.

The Mars Climate Orbiter failure also underscored the need for a cultural shift within NASA and its contractors. The incident highlighted the importance of fostering an environment where engineers and scientists feel empowered to question assumptions, raise concerns, and seek clarifications. Encouraging a culture of openness and transparency can help identify and rectify potential issues before they escalate into mission-critical problems.

Despite the loss of the Mars Climate Orbiter, NASA continued its exploration of Mars with other missions. The Mars Polar Lander, which was part of the same program, also ended in failure due to a different set of issues. However, subsequent missions such as the Mars Odyssey, launched in 2001, and the Mars Reconnaissance Orbiter, launched in 2005, successfully built upon the lessons learned from the earlier failures. These missions have provided invaluable data about Mars, significantly advancing our understanding of the Red Planet.

The Mars Climate Orbiter incident serves as a poignant reminder of the complexities and challenges inherent in space exploration. It highlights the critical importance of attention to detail, rigorous verification processes, effective communication, and adherence to established protocols. While the failure was a setback, the lessons learned have contributed to the continuous improvement of space mission planning, execution, and safety.

Chapter 16: The Vasa Warship Design Flaw

The Vasa warship disaster is a remarkable historical example of how design flaws, miscommunication, and a lack of proper testing can lead to catastrophic failure. The Vasa was a Swedish warship that sank on its maiden voyage in 1628. Despite being one of the most powerfully armed vessels of its time, it capsized and sank in Stockholm harbor, taking with it a significant portion of Sweden's naval hopes and financial investment. The Vasa's story highlights the importance of proper design principles, thorough testing, and the need for clear communication among all parties involved in a project.

The Vasa was commissioned by King Gustavus Adolphus of Sweden during the early 17th century, a time when Sweden was a rising power in Europe, engaged in various conflicts and wars. The king desired a powerful warship to bolster the Swedish navy and project Swedish power. The Vasa was intended to be the flagship of the fleet, symbolizing Sweden's naval strength and technological prowess. Designed to carry 64 bronze cannons and decorated with elaborate carvings, the ship was a formidable sight and a significant financial investment.

The construction of the Vasa began in 1626 under the supervision of Henrik Hybertsson, an experienced shipbuilder. However, the ship's design was altered multiple times during construction due to changes in royal directives and evolving requirements. One of the most significant changes was the decision to equip the Vasa with an unprecedented number of heavy cannons on two gun decks, a feature that had not been tried before on Swedish warships of this size. This decision dramatically increased the ship's weight and affected its stability.

The ship's design flaws were primarily rooted in its proportions. The Vasa was narrow and top-heavy, with a high center of gravity due to the heavy cannons mounted on the upper decks. The keel, which should have been longer and deeper to provide adequate stability, was relatively short and shallow. The ballast, which helps to stabilize a ship, was insufficient given the ship's top-heavy structure. These factors combined to make the Vasa extremely unstable and prone to capsizing.

Moreover, communication and decision-making issues exacerbated the design problems. King Gustavus Adolphus was heavily involved in the ship's design, often overriding the advice of experienced shipbuilders. The pressure to complete the ship quickly and the king's desire for a powerful, heavily armed vessel led to compromises in the ship's stability. Additionally, the king was away on military campaigns for much of the construction period, leaving key decisions to be made by subordinates who might not have had the necessary expertise or authority to challenge the king's directives.

A critical moment in the Vasa's construction was the stability test conducted in 1628. During this test, 30 men ran back and forth across the deck to simulate the ship's movement in the water. After only three runs, the test was stopped because the ship began to sway dangerously. Despite this clear indication of instability, the ship was not redesigned or sufficiently modified. This decision was likely influenced by the urgency to launch the ship and the reluctance to report negative findings that could delay the project further.

The Vasa set sail on August 10, 1628, on its maiden voyage. The ship had not traveled more than a nautical mile from the dock when it encountered a strong gust of wind. The wind caused the Vasa to heel over to one side, and water began to flood through the open gun ports. The ship capsized quickly, sinking to the bottom of Stockholm harbor within minutes. Of the 150 people on board, around 30 to 50 perished in the disaster.

The aftermath of the Vasa's sinking was marked by investigations and attempts to assign blame. A commission was established to determine the cause of the disaster and hold those responsible accountable. However, the inquiry faced significant challenges, as it involved powerful individuals and the king's direct orders. Ultimately, no one was held accountable for the failure, and the focus shifted to salvaging what could be recovered from the wreck.

The Vasa remained at the bottom of Stockholm harbor for over 300 years until it was rediscovered and salvaged in the 1950s. The cold, brackish waters of the Baltic Sea had preserved the ship remarkably well. The Vasa was raised in 1961 and became a national symbol and a major tourist attraction. The ship is now housed in the Vasa Museum in Stockholm, where it serves as a poignant reminder of the consequences of poor design and inadequate testing.

The Vasa disaster has provided valuable lessons for modern engineering and project management. One of the key takeaways is the importance of adhering to sound design principles and ensuring that any design changes are thoroughly evaluated and tested. The decision to add an extra gun deck and additional cannons without properly considering the impact on the ship's stability was a critical mistake. Modern engineering practices emphasize the need for detailed simulations and testing to validate design choices and ensure safety.

Effective communication and decision-making are also crucial in large-scale projects. The Vasa's construction was hampered by a lack of clear communication and the overriding influence of non-expert decision-makers. In contemporary projects, it is essential to establish clear lines of communication and ensure that expert advice is heeded, even if it means challenging directives from higher authorities.

The Vasa incident also underscores the importance of thorough testing and validation. The stability test conducted on the Vasa indicated significant problems, but these warnings were not acted upon. Modern engineering projects incorporate rigorous testing protocols and a culture of safety that prioritizes addressing any identified issues before proceeding.

The preservation and study of the Vasa have provided historians and engineers with invaluable insights into 17th-century shipbuilding techniques and the challenges faced by early naval engineers. The ship's detailed carvings and construction methods have been meticulously documented, contributing to our understanding of historical craftsmanship and design practices. Additionally, the Vasa has become a case study in the importance of balancing ambitious goals with practical engineering constraints.

Chapter 17: The Space Shuttle Columbia Foam Strike

The Space Shuttle Columbia disaster of 2003 is one of the most tragic and instructive episodes in the history of space exploration. This disaster was caused by a seemingly minor event: a piece of foam insulation broke off from the external fuel tank during launch and struck the left wing of the shuttle. The resulting damage led to the destruction of Columbia upon re-entry into the Earth's atmosphere, killing all seven crew members. This event underscores the critical importance of attention to detail, thorough risk assessment, and a robust safety culture in complex engineering projects.

The Space Shuttle Columbia (OV-102) was the first space-rated orbiter in NASA's Space Shuttle fleet. It made its first flight in 1981 and successfully completed 27 missions before its final, ill-fated mission, STS-107. The primary goal of the STS-107 mission, which launched on January 16, 2003, was to conduct a variety of scientific experiments in orbit. The mission proceeded smoothly, with the crew carrying out their experiments and reporting no significant issues.

However, during the launch of STS-107, a piece of foam insulation from the external fuel tank detached and struck the leading edge of Columbia's left wing. This event was captured by ground-based cameras, but its significance was not fully understood at the time. The foam strike was not an unprecedented occurrence; similar events had been observed during previous shuttle launches without catastrophic consequences. Consequently, NASA engineers did not initially consider the foam strike to be a serious threat to the mission's safety.

The foam that struck Columbia's wing was part of the bipod ramp, a structure designed to reduce ice formation on the external fuel tank. The foam insulation was intended to prevent ice from forming and potentially detaching during launch, which could damage the shuttle.

However, the insulation itself could become a hazard if it detached, as it did in the case of STS-107. The piece of foam that struck Columbia was approximately the size of a briefcase and weighed about 1.67 pounds (0.76 kilograms).

As Columbia orbited the Earth, engineers on the ground reviewed the launch footage and became aware of the foam strike. Concerns were raised about potential damage to the thermal protection system (TPS) on the shuttle's left wing. The TPS, composed of reinforced carbon-carbon (RCC) panels and thermal tiles, was designed to protect the shuttle from the intense heat generated during re-entry into the Earth's atmosphere. Damage to this system could compromise the shuttle's structural integrity and endanger the crew.

In response to the concerns, NASA initiated an internal assessment to determine the potential impact of the foam strike. This assessment involved a series of simulations and analyses to estimate the extent of the damage. However, the analysis was hampered by several factors, including limited data and the inherent uncertainties in modeling the behavior of the foam and its impact on the TPS. Despite these challenges, the initial assessments suggested that the foam strike did not pose a significant threat to the mission.

One of the key decisions during this period was not to request high-resolution imagery of the shuttle in orbit, which could have provided a clearer understanding of the damage. There were several potential sources of such imagery, including military assets and other space-based platforms, but these options were not pursued. This decision was influenced by a combination of factors, including organizational culture, communication breakdowns, and the perception that the foam strike was not a critical issue.

The culture within NASA at the time played a significant role in the handling of the foam strike. There was a prevailing sense of confidence in the shuttle program and its safety measures, bolstered by the successful completion of numerous missions despite similar foam strikes. This sense of complacency contributed to a reluctance to challenge existing assumptions and a tendency to downplay potential risks. Additionally, there were organizational barriers that impeded effective communication and the escalation of concerns within NASA.

As the STS-107 mission continued, the crew remained unaware of the potential danger posed by the foam strike. They diligently carried out their scientific experiments and prepared for re-entry, confident in the shuttle's safety and reliability. The mission's scientific achievements included a range of experiments in microgravity, covering fields such as biology, physics, and materials science.

On February 1, 2003, Columbia began its re-entry into the Earth's atmosphere. As the shuttle descended, the damage to the left wing became critical. Superheated air entered the wing's structure, causing a rapid increase in temperature and the eventual structural failure of the wing. The shuttle began to break apart, and at approximately 9:00 AM EST, Columbia disintegrated over Texas and Louisiana. All seven crew members—Rick D. Husband, William C. McCool, Michael P. Anderson, Ilan Ramon, Kalpana Chawla, David M. Brown, and Laurel B. Clark—were killed.

The loss of Columbia and its crew was a devastating blow to NASA and the global space community. In the aftermath, NASA initiated a comprehensive investigation to determine the causes of the disaster and prevent future occurrences. The Columbia Accident Investigation Board (CAIB) was established to lead this effort, conducting an extensive review of the technical, organizational, and cultural factors that contributed to the accident.

The CAIB's final report, released in August 2003, identified the foam strike as the direct cause of the disaster. The report also highlighted several contributing factors, including the design of the external fuel tank, the decision-making processes within NASA, and the agency's safety culture. The investigation revealed that the foam insulation had detached due to a combination of factors, including the materials used, the tank's design, and the conditions during launch.

One of the critical findings of the CAIB was the need for significant changes in NASA's organizational culture and safety practices. The report emphasized the importance of fostering an environment where concerns can be raised and addressed without fear of retribution. It also called for improvements in communication, decision-making, and risk assessment processes. These recommendations were aimed at ensuring that safety considerations were prioritized and that potential risks were thoroughly evaluated and mitigated.

In response to the CAIB's findings, NASA implemented a series of reforms to address the issues identified. These included redesigning the external fuel tank to reduce the risk of foam detachment, enhancing the shuttle's inspection and repair capabilities, and improving communication and decision-making processes. Additionally, NASA established the NASA Engineering and Safety Center (NESC) to provide independent technical assessments and ensure that safety remained a top priority in all missions.

The legacy of the Columbia disaster extends beyond the technical and organizational changes at NASA. The loss of Columbia and its crew had a profound impact on the global space community, underscoring the inherent risks of space exploration and the importance of continuous improvement in safety practices. The disaster also served as a stark reminder of the need for vigilance, transparency, and accountability in managing complex engineering projects.

In the years following the Columbia disaster, NASA successfully resumed shuttle flights and completed the assembly of the International Space Station (ISS). The lessons learned from the Columbia incident have informed subsequent missions and contributed to the development of safer and more reliable space systems. The emphasis on safety, risk management, and organizational culture continues to shape NASA's approach to space exploration and mission planning.

The Columbia disaster also had a lasting impact on the families of the crew members and the broader public. Memorials and tributes to the fallen astronauts serve as reminders of their sacrifice and dedication to the pursuit of knowledge and exploration. The disaster has inspired a renewed commitment to honoring their legacy through continued advancements in space exploration and the pursuit of scientific discovery.

Chapter 18: The 1979 Three Mile Island Partial Meltdown

The 1979 Three Mile Island partial meltdown is a significant event in the history of nuclear energy, serving as a stark reminder of the potential dangers associated with nuclear power and the importance of stringent safety measures, effective communication, and proper training. The incident occurred at the Three Mile Island Nuclear Generating Station in Dauphin County, Pennsylvania, on March 28, 1979. It was the most serious accident in the history of the American commercial nuclear power generating industry and had far-reaching implications for nuclear policy, public perception, and regulatory practices.

The Three Mile Island Nuclear Generating Station consisted of two pressurized water reactors (PWRs), designated TMI-1 and TMI-2. The plant was owned and operated by Metropolitan Edison (Met-Ed), a subsidiary of General Public Utilities (GPU). TMI-2, the reactor involved in the incident, was a relatively new reactor, having been brought online in December 1978. The plant was designed with multiple safety systems to manage emergencies, but on that fateful day, a combination of equipment malfunctions, design-related problems, and human errors led to a partial meltdown of the reactor core.

The incident began at 4:00 AM on March 28, when the secondary cooling circuit, which removes heat from the reactor core and transfers it to the steam generators, experienced a malfunction. This malfunction caused the primary cooling system, responsible for directly cooling the reactor core, to become overloaded. The main feedwater pumps, which supply water to the steam generators, stopped operating, and the turbine and reactor automatically shut down. This sequence of events triggered a rapid increase in pressure within the primary coolant system.

To alleviate the rising pressure, the pilot-operated relief valve (PORV) on the reactor's pressurizer opened as designed. However, the valve failed to close after the pressure was reduced, and this critical malfunction went unnoticed by the plant operators. As a result, large amounts of coolant continued to escape from the primary system, leading to a loss of coolant accident (LOCA). The continued loss of coolant caused the reactor core to overheat, eventually resulting in the partial meltdown of the fuel rods.

Compounding the problem was the fact that the control room operators received confusing and contradictory information from their instrumentation and control systems. The indicators suggested that the PORV was closed, when in fact it remained open. Consequently, the operators misinterpreted the situation and took actions that exacerbated the cooling problem. For instance, they reduced the flow of emergency cooling water, fearing that the pressurizer might become waterlogged. This decision, made based on incorrect information, further deprived the reactor core of necessary cooling and allowed the temperatures to rise dangerously high.

As the coolant levels in the reactor dropped, parts of the fuel rods were exposed, leading to the formation of a hydrogen gas bubble within the reactor vessel. The core's temperature reached around 4,000 degrees Fahrenheit, causing significant damage to the fuel rods and the release of radioactive materials into the reactor coolant. The hydrogen bubble posed a significant risk, as it could potentially explode if ignited, leading to catastrophic consequences. However, it was later determined that the bubble did not reach an explosive concentration.

The crisis continued for several hours, with plant operators struggling to understand the full extent of the situation and respond appropriately. By the afternoon of March 28, they managed to establish a stable cooling process and began to reduce the temperature and pressure within the reactor. It wasn't until nearly a week later that the reactor was brought to a cold shutdown state, marking the end of the immediate crisis.

Despite the seriousness of the partial meltdown, the containment building effectively contained most of the radioactive materials, preventing a significant release into the environment. However, a small amount of radioactive gases was released into the atmosphere, causing public concern and fear. The release was estimated to be around 13 million curies of radioactive noble gases, primarily xenon and krypton, but the exposure levels to the public were deemed to be minimal and not a significant health risk according to subsequent studies.

The Three Mile Island incident had profound implications for the nuclear industry and regulatory bodies. In the immediate aftermath, the public reaction was one of fear and skepticism regarding the safety of nuclear power. The incident led to the evacuation of pregnant women and young children from the surrounding areas, and the media coverage fueled widespread anxiety and opposition to nuclear energy.

The investigation into the incident was extensive and resulted in several key findings. One of the major issues identified was the lack of adequate training and preparedness of the plant operators to handle such a complex emergency. The control room design and the instrumentation were also found to be problematic, providing misleading information that contributed to the operators' incorrect decisions. Additionally, the design flaws in the PORV and the emergency cooling system were highlighted as critical factors that exacerbated the situation.

The Nuclear Regulatory Commission (NRC), the federal agency responsible for regulating nuclear power plants in the United States, took significant steps in response to the findings. The NRC conducted a thorough review of the incident and implemented numerous regulatory changes aimed at improving the safety and reliability of nuclear power plants. These changes included stricter requirements for operator training, enhancements to control room instrumentation and design, and improved emergency response procedures.

One of the lasting legacies of the Three Mile Island incident was the establishment of the Institute of Nuclear Power Operations (INPO) in 1979. INPO was created by the nuclear industry to promote the highest levels of safety and reliability in the operation of nuclear power plants. The organization developed comprehensive guidelines and training programs to ensure that plant operators were better prepared to handle emergencies and to foster a culture of safety within the industry.

The incident also had a profound impact on the construction and licensing of new nuclear power plants in the United States. The Three Mile Island accident significantly slowed the growth of the nuclear industry, leading to the cancellation or delay of many planned nuclear power projects. Public opposition to nuclear power increased, and the regulatory environment became more stringent, making it more challenging and costly to develop new nuclear facilities.

Over the years, extensive studies have been conducted to assess the long-term health effects of the Three Mile Island incident on the surrounding population. The majority of these studies have concluded that there were no significant adverse health impacts attributable to the incident. However, the psychological and social effects on the local community were considerable, with many residents experiencing anxiety and stress related to the perceived risks of radiation exposure.

In the decades following the incident, the damaged TMI-2 reactor remained in a state of monitored storage, and various plans were considered for its decommissioning. The cleanup and decontamination efforts were complex and costly, involving the removal of radioactive materials and the dismantling of damaged components. In 1993, the damaged reactor vessel was defueled, and the spent fuel was shipped to a storage facility. The site continued to be monitored for residual radiation and environmental safety.

The Three Mile Island incident serves as a case study in the importance of robust safety systems, effective operator training, and a culture of safety in the operation of nuclear power plants. It underscores the need for comprehensive risk assessment, thorough testing of safety equipment, and clear, accurate communication within the control room. The lessons learned from this incident have been incorporated into nuclear safety protocols worldwide, contributing to the development of safer and more resilient nuclear power plants.

Chapter 19: The Costa Concordia Captain's Mistake

The Costa Concordia disaster, a maritime tragedy that occurred on January 13, 2012, off the coast of Italy, is a prime example of how a seemingly minor error can lead to catastrophic consequences. The luxury cruise ship, owned by Costa Crociere and carrying more than 4,200 passengers and crew, set sail from Civitavecchia, Italy, on what was intended to be a leisurely Mediterranean voyage. However, this journey took a disastrous turn due to a series of critical errors made by the ship's captain, Francesco Schettino.

Captain Schettino, an experienced mariner with years of service, decided to perform a "salute" maneuver, an age-old maritime tradition where a ship sails close to the shore to greet onlookers. This particular salute was intended for the island of Giglio, a picturesque location known for its scenic beauty. The captain's decision to navigate the massive vessel so close to the island was influenced by a combination of factors, including a desire to impress both passengers and friends onshore. Despite the potential risks, he assured the crew that it was safe, relying on his expertise and the ship's advanced navigational systems.

However, Schettino's judgment was flawed. As the Costa Concordia approached Giglio, it veered dangerously close to the shoreline. The captain underestimated the ship's proximity to underwater rocks, which were not adequately charted on the navigational maps he used. At 9:45 PM, the ship struck a reef known as Le Scole, tearing a 160-foot gash in its hull. The impact was immediate and severe, causing the vessel to list rapidly and take on water.

The situation quickly escalated from a controlled maneuver to a full-blown emergency. Passengers were thrown into a state of panic as the ship lost power and the lights went out. The crew, unprepared for such an event, struggled to manage the crisis. Communication between the bridge and the rest of the ship broke down, exacerbating the chaos. Schettino's leadership was called into question as he failed to provide clear and decisive orders. Instead of coordinating an orderly evacuation, he hesitated and delayed the call to abandon ship.

Schettino's actions during the critical moments following the collision were widely criticized. He left the bridge and boarded a lifeboat while many passengers and crew members were still aboard the sinking vessel. This decision was seen as a grave dereliction of duty, violating maritime tradition and the captain's responsibility to ensure the safety of everyone on board. The evacuation process was chaotic and disorganized, with many lifeboats inaccessible due to the ship's severe list. Passengers reported confusion and fear as they tried to navigate the tilting decks and find a way off the ship.

The Costa Concordia disaster resulted in the deaths of 32 people, with many more injured. The rescue operation, involving the Italian Coast Guard and numerous local vessels, was hampered by the ship's precarious position and the darkness of the night. Survivors recounted harrowing experiences of clinging to the sides of the ship, jumping into the cold sea, and being rescued by brave responders who risked their lives to save others. The incident left a lasting impact on the community of Giglio and the broader maritime industry.

In the aftermath, extensive investigations were conducted to understand the causes and consequences of the disaster. It was revealed that several factors contributed to the tragedy, including human error, inadequate safety protocols, and failures in crisis management. Schettino faced legal proceedings and was eventually found guilty of manslaughter, causing a maritime disaster, and abandoning ship. He was sentenced to 16 years in prison, a verdict that underscored the severity of his mistakes and their tragic outcomes.

The Costa Concordia disaster prompted significant changes in the cruise industry. Regulations and safety standards were scrutinized and revised to prevent similar incidents in the future. Training programs for crew members were enhanced to ensure better preparedness for emergencies. The disaster also highlighted the importance of effective leadership and communication in crisis situations, emphasizing that the actions of individuals in critical moments can have far-reaching consequences.

The wreck of the Costa Concordia remained a poignant reminder of the disaster for years. The salvage operation to remove the ship, one of the most complex and expensive in maritime history, took over two years to complete. Engineers and divers worked tirelessly to stabilize, refloat, and eventually tow the vessel to a scrapyard. The process was a technical marvel, demonstrating human ingenuity and determination in the face of adversity.

In the broader context of maritime history, the Costa Concordia disaster serves as a cautionary tale. It illustrates how complacency, overconfidence, and a lack of adherence to safety protocols can lead to devastating outcomes. The tragedy also underscores the critical role of leadership and accountability in ensuring the safety of passengers and crew. While the Costa Concordia has been dismantled and removed from the waters of Giglio, the lessons learned from this disaster continue to resonate within the maritime community and beyond.

Chapter 20: The Piper Alpha Platform Fire

The Piper Alpha disaster, one of the most devastating offshore oil platform accidents in history, occurred on July 6, 1988, in the North Sea, approximately 120 miles northeast of Aberdeen, Scotland. This tragedy, resulting in the loss of 167 lives, highlighted the catastrophic consequences of a series of minor errors and systemic failures.

Piper Alpha, operated by Occidental Petroleum, was a large North Sea oil production platform. At its peak, it produced more than 300,000 barrels of crude oil per day, making it a crucial component of the UK's oil industry. The platform was a complex structure with multiple decks housing drilling operations, gas compression systems, and living quarters for the crew. The complexity of the platform's design played a significant role in the disaster that unfolded.

On the fateful day, routine maintenance was being conducted on a condensate pump in one of the gas compression modules. This maintenance required the removal of a pressure safety valve, which was crucial for preventing overpressure in the system. The valve was removed, and a blind flange was temporarily installed to seal the opening. However, due to a series of miscommunications, the blind flange was not properly secured. This oversight set the stage for the disaster.

The day shift ended, and the night shift took over without being adequately informed about the ongoing maintenance work and the status of the blind flange. Shortly after 9:00 PM, the pump that was supposed to remain offline was mistakenly started. This error caused gas condensate to leak from the unsecured blind flange, leading to a rapid buildup of highly flammable hydrocarbons. Within minutes, the leaked gas found an ignition source, triggering a massive explosion.

The initial explosion ripped through the platform, causing widespread destruction and igniting a series of fires. The force of the blast destroyed critical firefighting equipment and ruptured oil and gas pipelines, exacerbating the situation. The fire quickly spread to other parts of the platform, fueled by the vast amounts of oil and gas being processed. The intensity of the flames and the thick black smoke made it nearly impossible for the crew to control the blaze or organize an effective evacuation.

One of the most tragic aspects of the Piper Alpha disaster was the failure of the platform's emergency response systems. The explosion and subsequent fires knocked out the power supply, disabling communication systems and emergency alarms. This left the crew without any means to coordinate their actions or receive instructions. The platform's lifeboats and escape capsules were also rendered inaccessible by the spreading fires, trapping many workers in the inferno.

Survivors later recounted the harrowing moments as they attempted to escape the burning platform. Some managed to reach the lifeboat stations, only to find them engulfed in flames. Others were forced to jump into the sea from great heights, risking injury or death. The North Sea's frigid waters added another layer of peril, making survival for those who jumped extremely difficult. Rescue efforts were hindered by the chaos and the extreme conditions, with helicopters and standby vessels struggling to approach the platform.

The human toll was staggering. Out of the 226 people on board, only 61 survived. Many of the victims were found in the accommodation block, where they had taken refuge, believing it to be the safest place. However, the raging fires and lack of effective firefighting measures sealed their fate. The survivors were left with physical and emotional scars, having witnessed the deaths of their colleagues and friends in one of the worst offshore disasters ever recorded.

In the aftermath of the disaster, an extensive investigation was launched to determine the causes and identify the failures that led to the tragedy. The Cullen Inquiry, led by Lord Cullen, revealed a litany of safety lapses and regulatory shortcomings. It was found that the platform's design and safety systems were inadequate for dealing with such a catastrophic event. The inquiry also highlighted the lack of proper training and emergency preparedness among the crew, as well as poor communication and coordination between shifts.

One of the key findings was the failure to properly manage and document maintenance activities. The miscommunication regarding the status of the blind flange and the subsequent starting of the pump were identified as critical errors. The inquiry also pointed out that the platform's operator, Occidental Petroleum, had not fully implemented safety recommendations from previous incidents, indicating a systemic failure to prioritize safety.

The Cullen Report, published in 1990, made 106 recommendations aimed at improving offshore safety. These recommendations led to significant changes in the industry, including the establishment of the Offshore Safety Division within the Health and Safety Executive (HSE), the introduction of stricter safety regulations, and the requirement for operators to conduct thorough risk assessments and safety case studies. The disaster also prompted the development of better training programs for offshore workers and the enhancement of emergency response capabilities.

The legacy of the Piper Alpha disaster extends beyond regulatory changes. It served as a stark reminder of the importance of safety in high-risk industries and the devastating consequences of neglecting it. The lessons learned from this tragedy have been applied globally, influencing safety standards and practices in the oil and gas sector. Despite the improvements, the memory of Piper Alpha remains a sobering reminder of the potential for disaster and the need for constant vigilance and commitment to safety.

The site of the Piper Alpha platform was eventually cleared, and a memorial was erected in Aberdeen to honor the victims. Every year, on the anniversary of the disaster, families, survivors, and industry professionals gather to remember those who lost their lives and to reaffirm their dedication to preventing such tragedies in the future. The Piper Alpha disaster is not just a historical event; it is a symbol of the ongoing struggle to balance industrial progress with the imperative to protect human lives.

Chapter 21: The Great Boston Molasses Flood

The Great Boston Molasses Flood, a bizarre yet tragic event, took place on January 15, 1919, in the North End neighborhood of Boston, Massachusetts. It is remembered as one of the most unusual disasters in American history, where a massive storage tank containing over 2.3 million gallons of molasses burst, unleashing a deadly wave of thick, sticky syrup through the streets. This catastrophe resulted in 21 fatalities, numerous injuries, and extensive property damage, forever embedding itself in the annals of Boston's local history.

The story of the Great Boston Molasses Flood begins with the construction of the enormous storage tank by the United States Industrial Alcohol Company (USIA) in 1915. The tank was built to house molasses, which was used in the production of industrial alcohol—a key ingredient in munitions manufacturing during World War I. Located at 529 Commercial Street, near Keany Square, the tank was a towering structure, standing 50 feet high and 90 feet in diameter. However, from the outset, the construction of the tank was marred by shortcuts and substandard materials, raising concerns about its integrity.

Despite these issues, the tank was filled to capacity on several occasions without incident. However, residents of the North End reported strange noises and leaks, indicating that the tank was under considerable strain. These warning signs were largely ignored by USIA, who were more focused on meeting the high demand for industrial alcohol rather than addressing potential safety hazards.

On January 15, 1919, the temperature in Boston had risen rapidly from the freezing conditions of the previous days to an unseasonably warm 40 degrees Fahrenheit. The rapid temperature change is believed to have contributed to the disaster. At approximately 12:30 PM, the tank exploded with a thunderous roar, sending a tidal wave of molasses rushing through the streets at an estimated speed of 35 miles per hour. The initial force of the explosion was so powerful that rivets from the tank were propelled with the velocity of bullets, and the steel panels were ripped apart, creating shrapnel that added to the destruction.

The wave of molasses, standing 25 feet high at its peak, swept away everything in its path. Buildings were knocked off their foundations, and wooden homes were crushed under the immense pressure. The Engine 31 firehouse was destroyed, killing several firefighters who were inside. The molasses engulfed the neighborhood, trapping people and animals alike in its sticky, suffocating embrace. Eyewitnesses described the scene as a nightmarish landscape, with the dense syrup making it nearly impossible for victims to escape or be rescued.

Rescue efforts began almost immediately, but the molasses proved to be a formidable obstacle. The Boston Fire Department, Red Cross, police, and volunteers all converged on the scene, but they struggled to navigate the thick, treacherous terrain. Horses and wagons were rendered useless, and even motor vehicles found it difficult to move through the molasses. Many rescuers resorted to using makeshift boats and planks to reach those trapped in the sticky flood.

The human toll was devastating. Twenty-one people lost their lives, either through drowning, being crushed by debris, or asphyxiation. The victims ranged from children to laborers to firefighters, each caught unawares by the sudden catastrophe. In addition to the fatalities, about 150 people were injured, suffering from broken bones, concussions, and severe molasses burns. The physical aftermath was horrific, but the emotional and psychological scars left on survivors and rescuers were equally profound.

The cleanup operation was an arduous task that took weeks to complete. The molasses, which had quickly cooled and hardened, required extensive labor to remove. Workers used sand, salt water, and even fire hoses to try to dilute and wash away the syrup. Despite their efforts, the cleanup was a painstakingly slow process, and the molasses left a lingering presence, with the smell permeating the area for months. The Boston Harbor was stained brown until the summer, as the molasses had seeped into the water, causing environmental concerns.

In the aftermath of the disaster, investigations were launched to determine the cause and assign responsibility. It became evident that the USIA had been negligent in the construction and maintenance of the tank. Evidence showed that the tank had been poorly designed, with walls too thin to withstand the pressure of the molasses. Additionally, reports surfaced that the company had failed to conduct proper safety tests and ignored the numerous warning signs and complaints from residents.

The disaster led to a landmark legal case, with over 125 lawsuits filed against USIA. The litigation lasted for six years, culminating in a decision that held the company liable for the disaster. The court found that USIA had been reckless and negligent, awarding substantial damages to the victims and their families. This case set a significant precedent for corporate accountability and improved industrial safety standards.

The Great Boston Molasses Flood had far-reaching implications beyond the immediate tragedy. It underscored the importance of rigorous safety regulations and proper oversight in industrial practices. The disaster prompted changes in building codes and construction standards, particularly for large storage tanks, ensuring that similar accidents would be less likely to occur in the future. Moreover, it highlighted the need for companies to prioritize public safety over profit, a lesson that remains relevant to this day.

In Boston, the memory of the molasses flood endures as a poignant reminder of a dark chapter in the city's history. The site of the disaster, now home to a recreational complex and commercial buildings, bears little resemblance to the scene of devastation from 1919. However, plaques and memorials commemorate the event, ensuring that the stories of those who perished and those who survived are not forgotten. Each year, on the anniversary of the flood, locals and historians gather to reflect on the tragedy and the resilience of the North End community.

The Great Boston Molasses Flood remains an enduring symbol of the unexpected and far-reaching consequences of minor errors and negligence. The event continues to capture the imagination and curiosity of people worldwide, serving as a cautionary tale of how industrial progress and human oversight can intersect with tragic results. Despite its bizarre nature, the flood is a sobering reminder of the importance of vigilance, responsibility, and respect for the power of nature and industrial processes.

Chapter 22: The 2008 Financial Crisis Rating Oversight

The 2008 Financial Crisis, also known as the Global Financial Crisis (GFC), was a severe worldwide economic crisis that occurred in the late 2000s. It is widely regarded as the most serious financial crisis since the Great Depression. One of the critical factors contributing to the crisis was the failure of credit rating agencies to accurately assess the risks associated with mortgage-backed securities (MBS) and collateralized debt obligations (CDOs). The role of rating agencies and the oversight of their activities provide a crucial lens through which to understand the complexity and impact of the crisis.

Credit rating agencies such as Moody's, Standard & Poor's (S&P), and Fitch Ratings play a pivotal role in the financial markets. Their ratings are used to assess the creditworthiness of various financial instruments, including corporate bonds, government bonds, and structured financial products like MBS and CDOs. Investors rely heavily on these ratings to make informed decisions about the risk and return of their investments. However, during the years leading up to the 2008 Financial Crisis, the rating agencies failed to provide accurate and reliable assessments of the risks associated with these structured products.

The housing boom of the early 2000s was characterized by a rapid increase in home prices and a surge in mortgage lending, including subprime mortgages—loans made to borrowers with poor credit histories. Financial institutions pooled these mortgages into MBS and CDOs, which were then sold to investors. These complex financial products were often highly rated by credit rating agencies, even though the underlying mortgages were risky. The high ratings were crucial in attracting a broad range of investors, including pension funds, insurance companies, and foreign governments, who were seeking safe investments with higher yields than traditional government bonds.

One of the primary reasons for the inflated ratings was the inherent conflict of interest within the credit rating industry. Rating agencies are paid by the issuers of the securities they rate, creating a potential bias towards providing favorable ratings. This "issuer-pays" model led to a situation where rating agencies competed for business by offering higher ratings, a practice known as "ratings shopping." Financial institutions would shop around for the best ratings, and agencies, eager to secure business, would often oblige. This conflict of interest undermined the objectivity and reliability of the ratings.

The methodologies used by rating agencies to assess the risk of MBS and CDOs were also flawed. These models relied heavily on historical data, which did not account for the possibility of a widespread decline in housing prices or a significant increase in mortgage defaults. The models assumed that housing prices would continue to rise or remain stable, an assumption that proved disastrously incorrect. When housing prices began to fall, and mortgage defaults increased, the underlying assumptions of the ratings were invalidated, leading to massive downgrades of these securities.

The lack of transparency in the rating process further exacerbated the problem. Investors had limited insight into how the ratings were determined and the specific risks associated with the securities they were purchasing. The complexity of MBS and CDOs made it difficult for even sophisticated investors to fully understand their risk profile. The high ratings provided a false sense of security, leading many investors to underestimate the potential for loss.

As the housing market began to collapse in 2007, the true risk of MBS and CDOs became apparent. The downgrades of these securities triggered a cascade of financial distress. Financial institutions that held large quantities of MBS and CDOs suffered significant losses, leading to a liquidity crisis as they struggled to meet their obligations. The interconnectedness of the financial system meant that the problems quickly spread, affecting banks, insurance companies, and investment funds worldwide.

One of the most notable examples of the impact of the crisis was the collapse of Lehman Brothers in September 2008. Lehman Brothers, a major investment bank, was heavily exposed to MBS and CDOs. The firm's bankruptcy sent shockwaves through the financial markets, leading to a severe tightening of credit and a loss of confidence in the financial system. Other financial institutions, such as Bear Stearns, Merrill Lynch, and AIG, also faced significant distress, requiring government intervention to prevent their collapse.

The crisis prompted a series of government bailouts and emergency measures aimed at stabilizing the financial system. The U.S. government, through the Troubled Asset Relief Program (TARP), injected capital into banks to restore confidence and provide liquidity. Central banks around the world lowered interest rates and provided emergency funding to support financial institutions. Despite these efforts, the crisis led to a deep recession, with millions of people losing their jobs and homes.

In the aftermath of the crisis, there was a widespread recognition of the need for regulatory reform to address the failures of the credit rating agencies and the broader financial system. The Dodd-Frank Wall Street Reform and Consumer Protection Act, passed in 2010, included provisions aimed at increasing oversight and accountability of rating agencies. The Act created the Office of Credit Ratings within the Securities and Exchange Commission (SEC) to oversee the activities of rating agencies and ensure they follow established standards and procedures.

Dodd-Frank also sought to address the conflict of interest inherent in the issuer-pays model. It mandated greater transparency in the rating process, requiring agencies to disclose the methodologies and assumptions used to determine ratings. The Act also allowed investors to sue rating agencies for knowingly or recklessly issuing inaccurate ratings, providing a legal avenue for accountability.

Despite these reforms, challenges remain in the credit rating industry. The issuer-pays model is still in place, and questions about the objectivity and reliability of ratings persist. The complexity of financial products continues to pose challenges for accurate risk assessment. While regulatory oversight has increased, ensuring the independence and effectiveness of rating agencies remains a critical issue.

The 2008 Financial Crisis highlighted the systemic risks posed by the failure of rating agencies to accurately assess the risk of financial products. It underscored the need for robust regulatory frameworks, transparency, and accountability to ensure the stability of the financial system. The lessons learned from the crisis continue to inform financial regulation and oversight, with the aim of preventing a similar catastrophe in the future.

The impact of the crisis was felt not only in the financial markets but also in the broader economy. The resulting recession led to significant economic hardship, with millions of people losing their jobs, homes, and savings. The social and political consequences of the crisis were profound, contributing to increased skepticism towards financial institutions and regulatory bodies. The crisis also prompted a reevaluation of economic policies and the role of government in regulating markets and ensuring financial stability.

The story of the 2008 Financial Crisis and the role of rating agencies serves as a cautionary tale about the dangers of unchecked financial innovation, conflicts of interest, and inadequate regulatory oversight. It highlights the importance of maintaining vigilance and ensuring that the financial system operates in a manner that promotes stability, transparency, and fairness. The reforms implemented in the wake of the crisis are a step towards achieving these goals, but the ongoing challenges underscore the need for continued efforts to strengthen the resilience of the financial system.

Chapter 23: The Johnstown Flood of 1889

The Johnstown Flood of 1889, also known as the Great Flood, was a catastrophic event that occurred on May 31, 1889, in Johnstown, Pennsylvania. It is one of the most devastating floods in American history, resulting in the deaths of over 2,200 people and causing widespread destruction. The disaster was a consequence of a combination of natural and man-made factors, including heavy rainfall, poor maintenance of the South Fork Dam, and the socio-economic conditions of the time.

Johnstown, located in a narrow valley at the confluence of the Little Conemaugh River and Stony Creek, was a thriving industrial town by the late 19th century. It was home to the Cambria Iron Works, one of the largest steel mills in the United States. The town's prosperity attracted a substantial population, making it a bustling hub of activity. However, Johnstown's location in a flood-prone valley, coupled with the deforestation and industrial development in the region, made it particularly vulnerable to flooding.

The South Fork Dam, situated approximately 14 miles upstream of Johnstown, was originally constructed in the early 1850s as part of the Pennsylvania Mainline Canal system. The dam was intended to create the Conemaugh Lake, a reservoir to supply water to the canal. However, the canal system became obsolete with the advent of the railroads, and the dam fell into disrepair. In the 1880s, the dam and reservoir were acquired by a group of wealthy industrialists from Pittsburgh, who formed the South Fork Fishing and Hunting Club. They repaired the dam to create a private resort, but their repairs were substandard, and they made several modifications that weakened the structure.

One of the most critical modifications was the lowering of the dam to accommodate a road across its top. This reduction in height significantly reduced the dam's ability to hold back water during periods of heavy rainfall. Additionally, the club members installed fish screens on the spillway to prevent the loss of fish from their private lake. These screens frequently became clogged with debris, further compromising the dam's ability to manage excess water.

In the days leading up to the disaster, the region experienced an unusually intense storm that brought heavy rainfall. The ground was already saturated from previous rains, and the additional deluge caused rivers and streams to swell rapidly. On the morning of May 31, 1889, the situation became critical as water levels in the Conemaugh Lake rose dangerously close to the top of the dam. Despite efforts by the South Fork Fishing and Hunting Club's caretaker and other workers to reinforce the dam with mud, rocks, and other materials, it became clear that the structure was at imminent risk of failure.

At approximately 3:10 PM, the South Fork Dam breached, releasing an estimated 20 million tons of water in a massive wave down the narrow valley. The wall of water, reported to be as high as 60 feet, traveled at speeds of up to 40 miles per hour, obliterating everything in its path. The floodwaters first struck the small communities of South Fork, Mineral Point, East Conemaugh, and Woodvale, causing extensive destruction and loss of life.

As the floodwaters roared towards Johnstown, they picked up debris, including trees, houses, railroad cars, and even locomotives, transforming into a deadly torrent. The residents of Johnstown had little time to react. Some had received warnings, but the severity of the situation was underestimated by many. By the time the flood hit Johnstown at around 4:07 PM, it was an unstoppable force, leveling buildings, uprooting infrastructure, and sweeping away people, animals, and entire families.

The aftermath of the flood was a scene of utter devastation. Johnstown and its surrounding areas were left in ruins, buried under a thick layer of mud and debris. The official death toll was over 2,200, but the exact number of casualties is likely higher, as many bodies were never recovered. The disaster also caused significant economic damage, estimated at around $17 million at the time (equivalent to roughly $500 million today). Homes, factories, and businesses were destroyed, leaving thousands of people homeless and without livelihoods.

The response to the disaster was swift and extensive. News of the flood spread rapidly, and relief efforts were mobilized from across the country. Clara Barton, the founder of the American Red Cross, led one of the first major disaster relief operations in the organization's history. She and her team arrived in Johnstown within days and provided critical assistance, including medical care, food, clothing, and shelter to the survivors. The relief efforts lasted for months, and the American Red Cross's work in Johnstown set a precedent for future disaster response.

The Johnstown Flood also had significant legal and social repercussions. Public outrage over the role of the South Fork Fishing and Hunting Club and its members in the disaster was widespread. Many blamed the club for neglecting the maintenance of the dam and prioritizing their private interests over public safety. Despite numerous lawsuits filed against the club and its wealthy members, they were never held legally accountable. The courts ruled that the disaster was an "act of God," and the plaintiffs were unable to prove negligence. This outcome highlighted the limitations of the legal system in addressing corporate and individual responsibility in such catastrophic events.

The flood also brought attention to the need for better engineering practices and oversight of infrastructure projects. The disaster underscored the importance of proper design, construction, and maintenance of dams and other critical structures. In the years following the flood, there were calls for stricter regulations and improved safety standards to prevent similar tragedies.

In Johnstown, the community's resilience and determination to rebuild were evident in the months and years following the flood. The town was gradually reconstructed, with new homes, businesses, and infrastructure replacing what had been lost. Memorials were erected to honor the victims, including the Grandview Cemetery, where many of the flood's victims were buried. The Johnstown Flood Museum, established later, serves as a poignant reminder of the disaster and a testament to the enduring spirit of the community.

The legacy of the Johnstown Flood of 1889 extends beyond the immediate aftermath of the disaster. It serves as a powerful reminder of the potential consequences of human negligence and the importance of responsible management of natural and man-made resources. The flood also highlighted the need for effective disaster response and relief efforts, setting a standard for future humanitarian operations.

The Johnstown Flood remains a significant event in American history, remembered for its tragic loss of life, the heroism of those who responded to the disaster, and the lessons it imparted about engineering, legal responsibility, and community resilience. The story of the flood continues to be studied and commemorated, ensuring that the memory of those who perished and the impact of the disaster on Johnstown and beyond are not forgotten.

Chapter 24: The Sinking of the Lusitania

The sinking of the RMS Lusitania on May 7, 1915, stands as one of the pivotal maritime disasters of the 20th century, an event that not only shocked the world but also had far-reaching implications for international relations and the course of World War I. The Lusitania, a British ocean liner, was en route from New York to Liverpool when it was torpedoed by a German U-boat, U-20, off the southern coast of Ireland. The attack resulted in the deaths of 1,198 of the 1,959 people on board, including 128 Americans, which played a crucial role in swaying public opinion in the United States and ultimately contributing to its entry into the war.

The Lusitania was one of the largest and fastest passenger ships of its time, operated by the Cunard Line. Launched in 1906, it was designed to compete with the German liners for the prestigious Blue Riband, awarded for the fastest transatlantic crossing. The Lusitania was renowned for its luxurious accommodations and cutting-edge technology, including its four turbine engines, which enabled it to maintain a high speed of 25 knots. This made it an attractive choice for passengers seeking a swift and comfortable journey across the Atlantic.

By 1915, the First World War had been raging for nearly a year, and the seas around the British Isles had become a dangerous theater of war. Germany had declared the waters around Britain a war zone and warned that Allied ships, including civilian vessels, were at risk of being sunk by their submarines. Despite this, the Lusitania continued its transatlantic service, carrying not only passengers but also cargo, including munitions and other war supplies, a fact that was kept secret from most of the passengers.

On May 1, 1915, the Lusitania departed from Pier 54 in New York City on its voyage to Liverpool. Among the passengers were a mix of British citizens, Americans, and other nationals, including businessmen, tourists, and families. The ship's captain, William

Thomas Turner, was an experienced mariner who was aware of the dangers posed by German U-boats. Despite warnings from the German Embassy published in American newspapers, advising passengers not to travel on British ships, many believed that the Lusitania's speed and the short distance it had left to travel in British waters would ensure its safety.

As the Lusitania approached the coast of Ireland on May 7, it entered an area known for U-boat activity. U-20, commanded by Kapitänleutnant Walther Schwieger, had been patrolling the waters and had already sunk several ships in the preceding days. At around 2:10 PM, Schwieger spotted the Lusitania and decided to attack. He fired a single torpedo, which struck the ship on the starboard side, near the bow. The explosion was followed by a second, much larger detonation, which many believe was caused by the ignition of munitions stored in the cargo hold.

The impact of the explosions was catastrophic. The Lusitania began to list heavily to starboard and started sinking rapidly by the bow. Captain Turner ordered the ship to head towards the Irish coast in an attempt to beach it, but the vessel's condition deteriorated too quickly. The lifeboats were difficult to launch due to the severe list, and many of them capsized or were damaged during the launch process. Within 18 minutes of the torpedo strike, the Lusitania had sunk beneath the waves, leaving hundreds of passengers and crew struggling in the cold waters of the Atlantic.

Rescue efforts were hampered by the remote location and the swiftness of the disaster. Local fishermen and a few rescue vessels managed to save some survivors, but many perished from exposure or drowning. The final death toll was 1,198, making it one of the deadliest maritime disasters in history.

The sinking of the Lusitania had immediate and profound repercussions. In Britain, it fueled anti-German sentiment and was used as powerful propaganda to rally public support for the war effort.

The British government and press labeled the attack as a barbaric act of war, emphasizing the loss of innocent lives, particularly the women and children who were among the victims.

In the United States, the reaction was one of outrage and shock. Although the country was officially neutral at the time, the death of 128 American citizens galvanized public opinion against Germany. President Woodrow Wilson faced immense pressure to take action, and the incident strained diplomatic relations between the United States and Germany. Initially, Wilson sought to maintain neutrality, urging a restrained response and diplomatic negotiations. He demanded that Germany cease unrestricted submarine warfare and ensure the safety of non-combatant ships.

Germany, in response, justified the attack by claiming that the Lusitania was carrying contraband munitions and thus was a legitimate military target. The German government argued that the British policy of arming merchant ships and using civilian vessels to transport war materials blurred the lines between civilian and military targets. Despite these justifications, the global condemnation of the attack forced Germany to modify its submarine warfare tactics temporarily. In September 1915, Germany agreed to the "Sussex Pledge," promising not to sink passenger ships without warning and ensuring the safety of passengers and crew.

However, the respite was short-lived. By early 1917, Germany resumed unrestricted submarine warfare, believing it was the only way to break the British blockade and win the war. This decision, coupled with the interception of the Zimmermann Telegram—in which Germany proposed a military alliance with Mexico against the United States—prompted Wilson to ask Congress for a declaration of war. On April 6, 1917, the United States entered World War I, marking a turning point in the conflict.

The legacy of the Lusitania's sinking extended beyond the immediate wartime context. The disaster highlighted the vulnerabilities of civilian shipping in wartime and the devastating impact of submarine warfare. It also underscored the importance of international maritime law and the need for clear rules governing the conduct of war at sea. The tragedy prompted changes in naval strategy and ship design, including the development of convoys to protect merchant vessels and improvements in lifeboat safety and emergency procedures.

In the years following the sinking, numerous investigations and inquiries were conducted to determine the causes and assign blame. The British Admiralty maintained that the ship had been unfairly targeted, while Germany continued to assert that the presence of munitions justified the attack. The precise nature of the second explosion remains a subject of debate among historians and experts. Some suggest it was caused by coal dust igniting in the ship's bunkers, while others believe it was the detonation of the munitions on board.

The Lusitania itself became a symbol of the human cost of war and the perils of modern naval conflict. Memorials were erected to honor the victims, including a monument in Cobh, Ireland, where many of the victims were buried. The wreck of the Lusitania, lying at a depth of approximately 300 feet off the coast of Ireland, has been the subject of numerous dives and explorations, yielding artifacts and insights into the final moments of the ship.

The cultural impact of the Lusitania's sinking was also significant. It inspired countless works of art, literature, and film, capturing the public's imagination and reflecting the broader themes of heroism, tragedy, and the brutal realities of war. The disaster was a poignant reminder of the fragile line between peace and conflict and the profound human suffering that can result from geopolitical decisions.

Chapter 25: The Grenfell Tower Fire Insulation Error

The Grenfell Tower fire, which occurred on June 14, 2017, in West London, stands as one of the most devastating residential fires in modern British history. The fire, which claimed 72 lives and left many more injured and homeless, was exacerbated by critical errors in building materials and safety measures, particularly the use of flammable insulation and cladding. Understanding the full scope of the disaster requires a detailed exploration of the building's history, the regulatory environment, the sequence of events on that tragic night, and the aftermath.

Grenfell Tower was a 24-story residential high-rise built in 1974 as part of the Lancaster West Estate in North Kensington. Initially designed to provide much-needed social housing, the tower contained 129 flats. Over the decades, it became home to a diverse community. By the 2010s, the building had begun to show signs of aging and required substantial refurbishment to meet modern standards. In 2012, a regeneration project was proposed, aiming to update the building's exterior and improve its energy efficiency and aesthetic appeal. The refurbishment, carried out between 2014 and 2016, included the installation of new windows, a heating system, and external cladding designed to improve insulation and reduce heating costs.

The cladding system chosen for Grenfell Tower consisted of aluminum composite material (ACM) panels with a polyethylene core, paired with polyisocyanurate (PIR) insulation boards. This combination was intended to enhance the building's thermal efficiency. However, both the ACM panels and PIR insulation are highly flammable. Despite this, they met the building regulations at the time, which allowed for their use in high-rise buildings, provided they were installed correctly and met certain safety standards.

On the night of June 14, 2017, a fire broke out in a fourth-floor flat, reportedly caused by an electrical fault in a refrigerator. The fire quickly spread from the kitchen to the exterior of the building, igniting the combustible cladding and insulation. The flames rapidly ascended the tower, engulfing it in less than an hour. The vertical spread of the fire was unprecedented, driven by the flammable materials used in the cladding system, which acted as a chimney, drawing the fire upwards.

Inside the tower, the situation deteriorated rapidly. Many residents were trapped in their flats, as the building's single stairwell became impassable due to thick smoke and intense heat. The "stay put" policy, which advises residents to remain in their apartments during a fire, assuming that the fire will be contained within the unit of origin, proved disastrous. The policy is based on the assumption that high-rise buildings are designed to prevent the spread of fire, a principle that failed catastrophically at Grenfell.

Firefighters arrived on the scene within minutes of the alarm being raised, but they faced overwhelming challenges. The scale and speed of the fire's spread were unlike anything they had encountered before. Many residents were unable to escape, and those who did were often forced to make harrowing decisions, including jumping from windows or attempting to navigate smoke-filled corridors. The London Fire Brigade, despite their heroic efforts, were hindered by a lack of suitable equipment, such as high-reaching ladders and aerial platforms, and the unexpected behavior of the fire.

The aftermath of the Grenfell Tower fire revealed a cascade of failures at multiple levels, from building design and material choice to regulatory oversight and emergency response. One of the most critical issues was the failure to properly test and certify the safety of the cladding system. Investigations revealed that the ACM panels with a polyethylene core were not suitable for use in high-rise buildings due to their flammability. The PIR insulation, which also contributed to the fire's spread, similarly failed to meet safety standards when subjected to real-world conditions.

The refurbishment project itself was fraught with cost-cutting measures and mismanagement. The decision to use cheaper, more flammable materials instead of fire-resistant alternatives was influenced by budget constraints and a lack of rigorous oversight. The regulatory framework governing building safety in the UK was also called into question. Despite existing regulations that should have prevented the use of such dangerous materials, enforcement and clarity were severely lacking. Building regulations were complex and open to interpretation, allowing dangerous practices to slip through the cracks.

Public inquiries and investigations into the fire revealed deep-seated issues within the building industry and regulatory bodies. The Hackitt Review, an independent review of building regulations and fire safety led by Dame Judith Hackitt, highlighted systemic failings and called for a major overhaul of the regulatory system. The review emphasized the need for a clearer, more stringent regulatory framework, better enforcement, and a shift towards a culture of safety within the construction and building management sectors.

The tragedy also exposed significant social and economic inequalities. Grenfell Tower was home to a predominantly low-income, multicultural community, many of whom had raised concerns about fire safety prior to the disaster. Their warnings went unheeded, reflecting a broader neglect of the needs and voices of marginalized communities. The fire brought to light the urgent need for greater accountability and responsiveness from housing authorities and government bodies to the concerns of residents.

In the wake of the fire, there was an outpouring of public grief and solidarity. Communities across London and the UK rallied to support the survivors, providing shelter, clothing, food, and emotional support. The government established a public inquiry to investigate the causes of the fire and ensure that lessons were learned to prevent such a disaster from happening again. The inquiry, led by Sir Martin Moore-Bick, was tasked with examining the events leading up to the fire, the adequacy of the building's refurbishment, the response of emergency services, and the role of various organizations involved.

The inquiry has revealed shocking details about the extent of negligence and incompetence involved. Testimonies from survivors, experts, and officials have painted a harrowing picture of a disaster that was both predictable and preventable. The evidence presented has shown that the materials used in the refurbishment were known to be dangerous, that there were significant failures in communication and coordination among the agencies responsible for the building's safety, and that the residents' concerns were systematically ignored.

The Grenfell Tower fire also had broader implications for building safety across the UK and internationally. In the wake of the disaster, it was discovered that hundreds of other high-rise buildings in the UK were clad in similar combustible materials, prompting urgent safety reviews and remediation efforts. The tragedy underscored the importance of rigorous building standards, thorough testing of materials, and robust fire safety measures.

In addition to regulatory changes, the fire prompted a societal reckoning with issues of inequality, justice, and the treatment of marginalized communities. Grenfell became a symbol of the consequences of neglect and the need for systemic change to ensure that all residents, regardless of their economic or social status, are protected and heard.

The legacy of the Grenfell Tower fire continues to resonate. Memorials and commemorations honor the victims and remind the public and policymakers of the ongoing need for vigilance and reform. Survivors and bereaved families continue to fight for justice, advocating for safer housing, accountability, and meaningful change.

Chapter 26: The 1965 Northeast Blackout

The 1965 Northeast Blackout remains one of the most significant power failures in the history of the United States, marking a pivotal moment in the evolution of the national power grid and highlighting vulnerabilities in the rapidly expanding network of electrical infrastructure. On November 9, 1965, a series of events culminated in a massive blackout that left over 30 million people across the Northeastern United States and parts of Canada without power for up to 13 hours. The blackout had far-reaching implications for the energy sector, leading to sweeping reforms and improvements in grid management and reliability.

The power failure began at 5:16 PM Eastern Standard Time when a single protective relay on a transmission line near the Sir Adam Beck Hydroelectric Power Station No. 2 in Queenston, Ontario, malfunctioned. This relay was designed to detect and isolate problems within the power grid, but a defect caused it to trip unnecessarily, interrupting the flow of electricity. The sudden loss of this crucial transmission line created an imbalance in the power system, which quickly cascaded through the interconnected grid.

At that time, the power grid in the Northeastern United States and Canada was a complex and interconnected system designed to ensure a reliable supply of electricity across a vast region. This interconnectedness meant that power could be shared and rerouted in case of localized issues, theoretically increasing reliability. However, this system also meant that problems could spread rapidly if not contained quickly and effectively. As the Beck relay tripped, the imbalance caused a chain reaction of failures in the grid.

The initial disturbance caused by the relay failure led to a domino effect. Power plants and transmission lines across the region became overloaded and started to shut down to protect themselves from damage. Within minutes, the blackout spread through Ontario and into New York, New Jersey, New England, and other parts of the Northeast. The rapid sequence of shutdowns resulted in a complete loss of power in major cities, including New York City, Boston, and Toronto.

The impact of the blackout was immediate and profound. In New York City, the lights went out just as the evening rush hour was beginning, plunging the city into darkness and causing widespread chaos. Subway trains stopped in their tracks, trapping thousands of commuters underground. Traffic lights went out, leading to massive traffic jams and accidents. People found themselves stranded in elevators and office buildings, unable to leave or contact anyone for help.

Despite the initial shock and confusion, the response from the public was remarkably calm and orderly. New Yorkers, often stereotyped as brash and impatient, displayed resilience and community spirit. People helped direct traffic, shared information, and assisted those in need. Volunteers, police officers, and firefighters worked tirelessly to manage the situation, providing assistance wherever it was needed. In Toronto, similar scenes played out, with citizens coming together to navigate the unexpected darkness.

Emergency services were quickly mobilized to address the most pressing issues caused by the blackout. Hospitals and other critical facilities switched to backup generators to maintain essential services. Police and fire departments increased patrols to ensure public safety and respond to emergencies. Radio stations, which were still operational on battery power, became crucial sources of information, keeping the public informed about the situation and providing guidance on how to stay safe.

The blackout lasted for up to 13 hours in some areas, with power being gradually restored through the night and into the following day.

As the lights came back on, the focus shifted to understanding what had caused such a widespread and severe outage. The investigation that followed revealed the critical role of the protective relay failure and the resulting cascade of problems throughout the interconnected grid.

The 1965 Northeast Blackout highlighted several key vulnerabilities in the power grid. One of the primary issues was the lack of adequate communication and coordination among the various utilities and power plants. The interconnected nature of the grid meant that problems in one area could quickly affect other parts of the system, but there were no effective mechanisms in place to manage such widespread disruptions. The blackout also exposed the limitations of existing technology and the need for more robust protective measures to prevent similar incidents in the future.

In response to the blackout, significant changes were made to improve the reliability and resilience of the power grid. One of the most important outcomes was the establishment of the North American Electric Reliability Corporation (NERC) in 1968. NERC was created to develop and enforce reliability standards for the bulk power system across the United States, Canada, and parts of Mexico. Its mission was to ensure the stability and security of the power grid and prevent future blackouts through improved planning, coordination, and communication.

Technological advancements also played a crucial role in enhancing grid reliability. Utilities began investing in more sophisticated monitoring and control systems, such as Supervisory Control and Data Acquisition (SCADA) systems, which allowed for real-time monitoring and management of the power grid. These systems enabled operators to detect and respond to problems more quickly, reducing the risk of widespread outages. Additionally, improvements in protective relays and other grid components helped to prevent the kind of cascading failures that led to the 1965 blackout.

The blackout also underscored the importance of maintaining adequate reserves of generation capacity and transmission capability. Utilities were encouraged to build more redundancy into their systems, ensuring that there were backup sources of power available in case of unexpected failures. This included the construction of additional power plants and transmission lines, as well as the development of more flexible and responsive grid management strategies.

Public awareness and preparedness for power outages were also improved in the wake of the blackout. Government agencies and utilities launched campaigns to educate the public about how to stay safe during outages and the importance of emergency preparedness. Communities were encouraged to develop local plans for dealing with power failures, including establishing communication networks and identifying resources that could be mobilized in case of an emergency.

The 1965 Northeast Blackout had a lasting impact on the energy sector, shaping policies and practices that continue to influence grid management today. It served as a wake-up call for the industry, demonstrating the need for greater vigilance, coordination, and investment in infrastructure. The lessons learned from the blackout helped to create a more resilient and reliable power grid, better equipped to handle the challenges of an increasingly complex and interconnected energy system.

In addition to the technical and regulatory changes, the blackout also had broader social and cultural implications. It highlighted the critical role of electricity in modern life and the vulnerabilities that come with dependence on technology. The experience of living without power, even for a short period, prompted many people to reflect on their reliance on electrical systems and the importance of resilience and adaptability in the face of unexpected challenges.

The blackout also fostered a sense of community and solidarity among those affected. The stories of people coming together to help each other during the crisis served as a reminder of the strength and resilience of communities in times of adversity. This spirit of cooperation and mutual support was a silver lining in an otherwise dark and challenging experience, leaving a lasting impression on those who lived through it.

Chapter 27: The Quebec Bridge Collapse

The Quebec Bridge collapse is one of the most infamous engineering failures in history, and it is particularly notable because it collapsed not once, but twice, resulting in significant loss of life and a reassessment of engineering practices. This tragedy offers an essential case study in the importance of rigorous design, testing, and quality control in engineering projects. The Quebec Bridge spans the Saint Lawrence River near the city of Quebec, Canada, and its construction was initially intended to improve transportation links and bolster economic development in the region.

The story of the Quebec Bridge begins in the late 19th century. The city of Quebec, located on the northern bank of the Saint Lawrence River, was growing rapidly, and there was a clear need for a bridge to facilitate transportation across the river. The idea of constructing a bridge was first proposed in the 1850s, but it was not until 1887 that serious plans began to take shape. In 1887, the Quebec Bridge Company was established to oversee the construction of a bridge that would span the river. The initial design was a suspension bridge, but this idea was later abandoned in favor of a cantilever bridge design, which was considered more suitable for the site's conditions.

The bridge's construction was a monumental task, requiring immense resources and expertise. The project was awarded to the Phoenix Bridge Company of Phoenixville, Pennsylvania, with the design being overseen by Theodore Cooper, a renowned bridge engineer. Cooper's reputation as an expert in the field gave confidence to the stakeholders involved in the project. The design called for a cantilever bridge with a central span of 1,800 feet, which would make it the longest cantilever span in the world at that time. The ambitious design was meant to showcase the latest advancements in engineering and bridge construction.

Construction of the Quebec Bridge began in earnest in 1904. The project faced several challenges from the outset, including difficult working conditions, the need for precise engineering calculations, and the immense scale of the structure. As work progressed, signs of trouble began to emerge. Reports of bending and distortion in some of the bridge's components raised concerns, but these issues were initially dismissed or downplayed. The pressures to complete the project on schedule and within budget led to a reluctance to thoroughly investigate and address these warning signs.

On August 29, 1907, disaster struck. At around 5:30 PM, as construction workers were nearing the completion of the bridge's southern half, the entire structure suddenly collapsed. The collapse resulted in the deaths of 75 workers, making it one of the deadliest bridge construction accidents in history. The failure was catastrophic, with the central span plunging into the river, taking with it a mass of twisted steel and debris. The immediate cause of the collapse was the failure of the bridge's lower chord members, which buckled under the weight of the structure.

The aftermath of the collapse led to an urgent and thorough investigation. A Royal Commission was established to determine the causes of the disaster. The investigation revealed a series of critical design and engineering errors. One of the primary issues was that the bridge's designers had significantly underestimated the weight of the structure. The original calculations had not adequately accounted for the increased loads, leading to excessive stresses on key components of the bridge. Furthermore, the decision to proceed with construction despite clear signs of structural distress reflected a failure of oversight and quality control.

The findings of the Royal Commission placed much of the blame on Theodore Cooper, the project's consulting engineer, who had failed to adequately address the warning signs and had allowed construction to proceed without making necessary corrections. The Phoenix Bridge

Company also faced scrutiny for its role in the flawed design and construction process. The collapse prompted a widespread reevaluation of engineering practices, particularly concerning the importance of accurate load calculations and the need for rigorous inspection and testing during construction.

Despite the tragedy, plans to build a bridge across the Saint Lawrence River were not abandoned. The importance of the bridge for transportation and economic development remained a driving factor. In 1913, a new design for the bridge was proposed, with the construction being overseen by the St. Lawrence Bridge Company. This time, greater emphasis was placed on safety and structural integrity. Lessons from the first collapse were incorporated into the new design, which included more conservative load estimates and improved quality control measures.

Construction of the new Quebec Bridge began in 1913, but the project was soon beset by another disaster. On September 11, 1916, as the central span was being hoisted into place, the span fell into the river, killing 13 workers. This second collapse further highlighted the challenges and risks associated with large-scale bridge construction. The immediate cause of this collapse was the failure of a casting that was part of the hoisting mechanism, underscoring the importance of robust engineering and construction practices.

Despite these setbacks, determination to complete the bridge remained strong. Following the second collapse, a comprehensive review of the design and construction methods was undertaken. The lessons learned from both collapses were rigorously applied, and more stringent safety protocols were implemented. The final construction phase saw the successful completion of the bridge, and the Quebec Bridge was officially opened to traffic on December 3, 1919. The completed bridge, with its central span of 1,800 feet, stood as a testament to human perseverance and engineering resilience.

The Quebec Bridge remains in use today, serving as a critical transportation link and a symbol of the engineering challenges and triumphs of the early 20th century. The bridge's legacy is multifaceted. On one hand, it serves as a stark reminder of the catastrophic consequences of engineering failures. On the other hand, it stands as a symbol of the ability to learn from mistakes and to apply those lessons to create safer and more reliable infrastructure.

In the years following the Quebec Bridge collapses, the field of civil engineering underwent significant advancements. The importance of thorough design review, accurate load calculations, and rigorous quality control became more widely recognized. Engineering education and professional practices evolved to emphasize these critical aspects, ensuring that future projects would be approached with greater caution and precision. The collapses also underscored the importance of communication and transparency in large-scale engineering projects, fostering a culture of accountability and safety that continues to shape the industry today.

Moreover, the Quebec Bridge collapses highlighted the human cost of engineering failures. The loss of life and the impact on the families and communities of the workers who perished in the disasters remain an indelible part of the bridge's history. Memorials and commemorations serve to honor the memory of those who lost their lives and to remind current and future generations of the importance of safety and vigilance in engineering endeavors.

The Quebec Bridge itself, standing tall over the Saint Lawrence River, is a powerful symbol of both the potential and the perils of engineering. It represents a turning point in the history of civil engineering, prompting a reevaluation of practices and the implementation of more robust standards. The bridge's story is a testament to the critical importance of learning from past mistakes and striving for continuous improvement in the pursuit of progress and safety.

Chapter 28: The Ford Pinto Fuel Tank Design Flaw

The Ford Pinto, introduced in the early 1970s, has become a case study in automotive safety, corporate ethics, and product liability. The subcompact car, designed to compete with imports such as the Volkswagen Beetle and Japanese models, was part of Ford Motor Company's effort to produce a lightweight, affordable vehicle. However, the Ford Pinto became infamous not for its affordability or performance but for a critical design flaw in its fuel tank that led to devastating fires in rear-end collisions. This flaw, combined with corporate decisions driven by cost-benefit analyses, resulted in significant controversy, lawsuits, and ultimately, a profound impact on automotive safety standards.

The Ford Pinto's fuel tank design flaw centered on the placement of the tank itself. Positioned between the rear axle and the bumper, the fuel tank was susceptible to rupture in the event of a rear-end collision. The proximity to the rear axle and the absence of a protective barrier meant that even moderate impacts could cause the tank to puncture, leading to fuel leaks. These leaks, when exposed to ignition sources such as sparks from metal striking metal, could result in catastrophic fires.

Ford's internal documents revealed that the company was aware of the potential danger posed by the Pinto's design. Crash tests conducted during the vehicle's development indicated that the fuel tank could rupture in collisions at speeds as low as 20 miles per hour. Despite these alarming results, Ford decided to proceed with the design, influenced by a cost-benefit analysis that prioritized financial considerations over safety improvements.

The infamous "Pinto Memo," a document uncovered during subsequent litigation, illustrated Ford's reasoning. The memo outlined the costs associated with redesigning the fuel tank versus the estimated costs of potential lawsuits resulting from accidents. The analysis concluded that it would be cheaper to settle lawsuits than to implement the safety modification. Ford estimated that the cost of redesigning and installing a protective barrier for the fuel tank would be approximately $11 per vehicle, which, when multiplied by the expected number of vehicles sold, would amount to around $137 million. In contrast, the projected cost of litigation and settlements was calculated to be around $49.5 million.

This cost-benefit approach, which placed a monetary value on human lives and safety, sparked outrage and raised ethical questions about corporate responsibility. Critics argued that Ford's decision-making process prioritized profits over the safety and well-being of its customers. The Pinto case became emblematic of the broader issue of how corporations weigh safety against costs and the ethical implications of such calculations.

The Pinto's safety issues came to public attention through a series of accidents and subsequent legal battles. One of the most notable cases involved a 1972 accident in Indiana, where a Ford Pinto stalled on a highway and was rear-ended by another vehicle. The collision caused the Pinto's fuel tank to rupture and ignite, resulting in the deaths of three teenage girls trapped inside the car. This tragic incident, along with others, led to a spate of lawsuits against Ford, bringing the issue of the Pinto's safety into the national spotlight.

The legal proceedings revealed damning evidence about Ford's knowledge of the fuel tank defect and the company's decision to prioritize cost savings over safety improvements. In 1977, investigative journalist Mark Dowie's article "Pinto Madness" in Mother Jones magazine further exposed the issue, detailing the findings of internal documents and crash test results that Ford had attempted to keep confidential. Dowie's article argued that Ford had knowingly placed an unsafe vehicle on the market, leading to preventable deaths and injuries.

The public outcry and legal pressure eventually forced the National Highway Traffic Safety Administration (NHTSA) to take action. In 1978, the NHTSA issued a recall for all 1971-1976 Ford Pintos, affecting approximately 1.5 million vehicles. The recall mandated the installation of protective reinforcements around the fuel tank to reduce the risk of rupture in rear-end collisions. Ford's compliance with the recall and the subsequent modifications helped to mitigate the immediate safety concerns, but the damage to the company's reputation was profound.

The Pinto case had lasting implications for automotive safety regulations and corporate accountability. It highlighted the need for more stringent safety standards and rigorous testing for all vehicles. The scandal also underscored the importance of transparency and ethical decision-making within corporations. In response to the Pinto controversy, there were calls for greater oversight of the automotive industry and for laws that would hold companies accountable for prioritizing profits over safety.

One significant outcome of the Pinto scandal was the advancement of federal safety regulations. The controversy contributed to the passage of the Motor Vehicle Safety Act, which established the NHTSA and empowered it to set and enforce safety standards for all motor vehicles sold in the United States. The NHTSA's mandate includes conducting vehicle crash tests, investigating safety defects, and issuing recalls when necessary. These measures aim to prevent future incidents like the Pinto disaster by ensuring that vehicles meet rigorous safety standards before they reach consumers.

The Ford Pinto case also served as a catalyst for the development of product liability law in the United States. The lawsuits filed against Ford set important legal precedents for holding manufacturers accountable for defective products that cause harm to consumers. The principle of "strict liability," which holds manufacturers liable for injuries caused by defects in their products regardless of negligence, became more firmly established as a result of the Pinto litigation. This legal framework incentivizes companies to prioritize safety in their product designs to avoid costly lawsuits and reputational damage.

In addition to legal and regulatory changes, the Pinto case had a profound impact on corporate culture and ethics. The scandal highlighted the dangers of relying solely on cost-benefit analyses when making decisions that affect public safety. It underscored the importance of ethical considerations and the need for companies to prioritize the well-being of their customers. In the aftermath of the Pinto scandal, many corporations reevaluated their approaches to product safety and implemented more robust ethical guidelines to ensure that financial considerations did not override safety concerns.

The Ford Pinto's legacy is a complex one, marked by tragedy, controversy, and significant changes in the automotive industry and corporate governance. The design flaw in the Pinto's fuel tank and the subsequent decisions made by Ford executives illustrate the potentially dire consequences of prioritizing profits over safety. The scandal serves as a cautionary tale for companies across industries, emphasizing the importance of ethical decision-making, transparency, and a commitment to consumer safety.

Chapter 29: The 2003 New York City Blackout

The 2003 New York City blackout was a major power outage that affected a vast portion of the northeastern and midwestern United States and parts of Canada. The blackout began on the afternoon of August 14, 2003, and lasted for up to four days in some areas, with significant impacts on daily life, the economy, and the infrastructure of the affected regions. This event, one of the largest power outages in history, highlighted the vulnerabilities and interdependencies of modern electrical grids and prompted widespread reevaluation of energy policies and grid management practices.

The origins of the blackout can be traced to a series of failures in the electrical grid, which began with the tripping of a power line in northern Ohio. The initial fault occurred at approximately 2:00 PM Eastern Daylight Time when a high-voltage power line near Cleveland brushed against overgrown trees, causing it to trip and shut down. Under normal circumstances, this type of incident would have been isolated and managed through a series of fail-safes and backup systems designed to maintain the stability of the grid. However, on that day, a combination of factors prevented these mechanisms from working effectively.

One critical factor was the inadequate trimming of vegetation around power lines, a common maintenance issue that can lead to disruptions. As the affected line in Ohio went offline, the electrical load it had been carrying was redistributed to nearby lines. This sudden shift in load created additional stress on the surrounding infrastructure. Compounding the problem was a lack of real-time communication and coordination between different regional grid operators, which led to delays in identifying and responding to the initial fault.

The situation rapidly escalated as additional power lines became overloaded and tripped offline in a domino effect. Within a short span of time, multiple transmission lines and power plants in Ohio were affected, creating a significant imbalance between supply and demand. This imbalance caused voltage fluctuations and frequency instability across the grid, further straining the system. The cascading failures spread beyond Ohio, affecting power plants and transmission lines in neighboring states and eventually reaching the interconnected grids of the northeastern United States and southeastern Canada.

By 4:10 PM, the blackout had engulfed major cities including New York, Toronto, Detroit, and Cleveland. Approximately 50 million people were suddenly without power. The impact on New York City was particularly dramatic, as the loss of electricity brought the bustling metropolis to a standstill. Subways, elevators, and traffic lights ceased to function, leaving millions of people stranded or forced to navigate the city on foot. Office buildings, shops, and residences were plunged into darkness, creating an eerie and disorienting atmosphere.

The blackout had immediate and far-reaching consequences. In New York City, the loss of power disrupted virtually every aspect of urban life. Public transportation came to a halt, stranding thousands of commuters in subway cars and stations. The outage occurred during the evening rush hour, exacerbating the chaos as people tried to make their way home without the aid of mass transit. Streets were clogged with traffic as drivers attempted to navigate without functioning traffic lights, leading to gridlock and numerous accidents.

Emergency services were stretched thin as they responded to a surge in calls for assistance. Firefighters, police officers, and medical personnel faced significant challenges as they worked to rescue people trapped in elevators, respond to fires, and address other emergencies. Hospitals had to rely on backup generators to maintain critical functions, but non-essential services were severely limited. The blackout also posed significant risks to public health, particularly for vulnerable populations such as the elderly and those dependent on medical equipment that required electricity.

Businesses suffered extensive losses due to the interruption of normal operations. Retail stores, restaurants, and other commercial establishments were forced to close, leading to lost revenue and spoiled perishable goods. The financial sector, concentrated in New York City, experienced disruptions as trading systems and communication networks went offline. The New York Stock Exchange and other financial markets were forced to halt trading, causing uncertainty and volatility in global markets.

The blackout also had a profound impact on the social fabric of the affected areas. In the absence of electricity, people turned to alternative sources of light and entertainment. Candles and flashlights became essential tools, and neighbors gathered outside to share information and support each other. Despite the initial chaos, the blackout fostered a sense of community and resilience as people adapted to the challenges posed by the outage.

One of the most remarkable aspects of the blackout was the response of the public. Despite the widespread disruption and inconvenience, incidents of crime and disorder remained relatively low. In New York City, which had experienced significant unrest during previous blackouts, the 2003 outage saw a largely peaceful and cooperative response from residents. This was attributed to effective emergency management, a visible presence of law enforcement, and a sense of solidarity among the affected population.

As power was gradually restored over the following days, the focus shifted to understanding the causes of the blackout and preventing future occurrences. An extensive investigation was launched, involving multiple agencies and stakeholders from the United States and Canada. The joint U.S.-Canada Power System Outage Task Force conducted a detailed analysis of the events leading up to the blackout and identified several key factors that contributed to the widespread outage.

The investigation revealed significant deficiencies in grid management practices and infrastructure maintenance. One of the primary findings was the lack of adequate tree trimming near power lines, which had initiated the cascade of failures. The investigation also highlighted shortcomings in real-time monitoring and communication between regional grid operators. The fragmented nature of the grid management system, with multiple independent operators overseeing different segments of the network, contributed to delays in identifying and responding to the initial fault.

In response to these findings, several measures were implemented to enhance the reliability and resilience of the electrical grid. One of the key recommendations was the establishment of the North American Electric Reliability Corporation (NERC) as the central authority responsible for overseeing the reliability of the interconnected grid. NERC was tasked with developing and enforcing mandatory reliability standards for grid operators, aimed at preventing future blackouts.

Additionally, significant investments were made in upgrading infrastructure and implementing advanced monitoring and control systems. Utilities were required to adopt more rigorous maintenance practices, including regular tree trimming and inspections of power lines. Real-time monitoring capabilities were enhanced to provide grid operators with better visibility into the state of the network and enable quicker responses to potential faults.

The blackout also underscored the importance of grid modernization and the integration of new technologies. The adoption of smart grid technologies, including automated sensors and advanced communication systems, became a priority to improve the resilience and efficiency of the electrical grid. These technologies enable more precise monitoring and control of the grid, allowing for quicker detection and isolation of faults to prevent cascading failures.

The 2003 blackout had lasting impacts on energy policy and the approach to managing critical infrastructure. It highlighted the interconnectedness and interdependencies of modern power systems, emphasizing the need for coordinated efforts to ensure the stability and reliability of the grid. The event served as a wake-up call for policymakers, utilities, and regulators, prompting a reevaluation of existing practices and the implementation of measures to enhance the resilience of the electrical grid.

Chapter 30: The Hyatt Regency Walkway Collapse

The Hyatt Regency Walkway Collapse is one of the most devastating structural failures in American history, resulting in the deaths of 114 people and injuries to over 200 others. This tragic event occurred on July 17, 1981, at the Hyatt Regency Hotel in Kansas City, Missouri, during a tea dance event that drew hundreds of guests to the hotel's atrium. The disaster was not only a catastrophic structural failure but also a landmark case that exposed significant flaws in engineering practices, construction oversight, and ethical standards within the industry.

The design of the Hyatt Regency Hotel included a spectacular multi-story atrium with suspended walkways that allowed guests to move between floors while offering a striking architectural feature. These walkways, suspended from the ceiling by steel rods, were a key part of the hotel's aesthetic appeal. However, the innovative design also introduced complex structural challenges that required meticulous engineering and construction practices.

The original design of the walkways called for continuous steel rods to run through the fourth-floor walkway and connect to the second-floor walkway, suspending both from the ceiling. This design meant that the rods had to bear the combined weight of both walkways and any dynamic loads from foot traffic. Unfortunately, a crucial modification to this design was made during construction. The design change involved using two sets of rods, with one set suspending the second-floor walkway from the fourth-floor walkway, which in turn was suspended from the ceiling. This seemingly minor alteration effectively doubled the load on the connection points supporting the fourth-floor walkway.

The change was made without a thorough analysis of its impact on the structural integrity of the walkways. Miscommunication and a lack of rigorous review processes contributed to the flawed design being implemented. The revised design was not subjected to the same level of scrutiny as the original, and critical calculations regarding load-bearing capacities were either overlooked or not adequately considered. This oversight set the stage for the catastrophic failure that would occur nearly a year after the hotel's opening.

On the evening of July 17, 1981, the hotel's atrium was filled with guests attending a tea dance event. Many attendees were gathered on the walkways, enjoying the view and the lively atmosphere. At approximately 7:05 PM, the fourth-floor walkway suddenly gave way, collapsing onto the second-floor walkway below. Both walkways then crashed into the crowded atrium floor, resulting in a massive pile of debris and trapping hundreds of people under the wreckage.

The collapse was immediate and violent, causing significant structural damage and a chaotic scene of devastation. Emergency responders arrived swiftly, but the rescue efforts were complicated by the sheer scale of the disaster and the precarious nature of the remaining structure. Rescuers had to navigate through unstable debris to reach survivors, all while fearing further collapses. The situation was further exacerbated by the ongoing risk of additional structural failures, making the rescue operation extremely perilous.

The aftermath of the collapse was harrowing. The death toll quickly rose as bodies were pulled from the rubble, and the number of injured overwhelmed local hospitals. Survivors recounted harrowing stories of being trapped beneath debris, unable to move, and listening to the cries of others around them. The psychological trauma for both survivors and rescuers was profound, leaving a lasting impact on all those involved.

In the wake of the disaster, an extensive investigation was launched to determine the cause of the collapse. The National Bureau of

Standards (now the National Institute of Standards and Technology, or NIST) conducted a thorough investigation, along with independent inquiries by engineering firms and other regulatory bodies. The findings were unequivocal: the walkway collapse was the result of a critical design flaw exacerbated by a failure to follow proper engineering and construction protocols.

The investigation revealed that the change from a single continuous rod design to the double-rod system significantly increased the load on the connectors supporting the fourth-floor walkway. The connectors were not designed to bear the added load, and over time, the stress on these critical points led to a catastrophic failure. The inquiry also highlighted several systemic issues within the engineering and construction processes, including inadequate communication between the design team and construction contractors, insufficient oversight, and a lack of rigorous review procedures for design changes.

Legal consequences followed the technical findings. Numerous lawsuits were filed by victims and their families, leading to a lengthy legal battle. The engineering firm responsible for the design, Gillum-Colaco International Inc., faced significant scrutiny and ultimately admitted to errors in their work. The firm's principals had their engineering licenses revoked, and substantial financial settlements were awarded to the victims and their families. The lawsuits also brought to light the need for stricter regulations and standards in engineering practices.

The collapse prompted widespread changes in engineering ethics, education, and practice. One of the most significant outcomes was the development of stricter codes and standards for structural engineering. These included more rigorous requirements for peer review and oversight of design changes, improved communication protocols between architects, engineers, and construction teams, and enhanced training and certification processes for engineers. The American Society of Civil Engineers (ASCE) and other professional organizations also revisited their codes of ethics to emphasize the paramount importance of public safety and the ethical responsibilities of engineers.

The Hyatt Regency Walkway Collapse also had a profound impact on engineering education. Engineering programs across the United States incorporated case studies of the disaster into their curricula, emphasizing the importance of ethical decision-making, attention to detail, and the critical need for thorough analysis and review processes in engineering work. The case became a staple in courses on structural engineering, ethics, and professional practice, serving as a powerful example of the potential consequences of negligence and miscommunication in engineering projects.

Moreover, the collapse highlighted the importance of maintaining and enforcing rigorous building codes and standards. Regulatory bodies and industry organizations worked to strengthen building codes to prevent similar failures in the future. These efforts included updating load-bearing requirements, improving standards for materials and construction practices, and enhancing the review and approval processes for structural designs. The lessons learned from the Hyatt Regency disaster became integral to the ongoing evolution of building codes and standards worldwide.

The human impact of the disaster cannot be overstated. The survivors and families of the victims endured unimaginable suffering and loss. Memorials and remembrance ceremonies have been held to honor those who lost their lives and to acknowledge the heroism of the emergency responders and rescuers who risked their lives to save others. The disaster left an indelible mark on the Kansas City community and the broader field of structural engineering, serving as a somber reminder of the importance of vigilance, integrity, and responsibility in engineering practice.

Chapter 31: The B-2 Bomber Crash Due to Sensor Failure

The B-2 bomber crash due to sensor failure on February 23, 2008, at Andersen Air Force Base in Guam stands as one of the most notable incidents in the history of the U.S. Air Force's stealth bomber program. The B-2 Spirit, an advanced strategic bomber known for its stealth capabilities and sophisticated design, is a critical component of the United States' long-range strike arsenal. This particular crash not only resulted in the loss of a $1.4 billion aircraft but also raised significant concerns about the reliability of advanced technology in critical military assets.

The B-2 Spirit, developed by Northrop Grumman, represents the pinnacle of stealth technology. It is designed to penetrate dense anti-aircraft defenses and deliver both conventional and nuclear weapons. The aircraft's unique flying wing design, combined with advanced materials and coatings, renders it nearly invisible to radar. This capability allows it to undertake missions that would be highly risky or impossible for other aircraft. However, the complexity and sophistication of the B-2 also mean that it relies heavily on a multitude of advanced systems and sensors to function correctly.

On the day of the crash, the B-2 bomber, tail number 89-0127 and named the "Spirit of Kansas," was preparing for a routine flight. The aircraft had undergone extensive maintenance prior to the flight, including the application of special coatings designed to maintain its stealth capabilities. As part of pre-flight preparations, the aircraft's systems were checked, including the Air Data System (ADS), which is crucial for providing the necessary flight data to the avionics and flight control systems.

The Air Data System includes sensors that measure various parameters such as airspeed, altitude, and angle of attack. These data points are vital for the aircraft's flight computers to maintain stable and controlled flight. On this occasion, however, the sensors had been exposed to moisture due to the humid conditions in Guam, and the heaters designed to keep the sensors dry and operational were not turned on, leading to erroneous data being fed to the flight control systems.

As the B-2 took off, the inaccurate data from the malfunctioning sensors caused a critical error in the aircraft's flight control system. The flight computers, receiving incorrect information about the aircraft's speed and angle of attack, attempted to adjust the flight surfaces to maintain what they interpreted as level flight. This resulted in a severe pitch-up immediately after takeoff, a situation that the pilots could not recover from despite their efforts.

The aircraft climbed steeply, reaching an angle that was unsustainable, leading to a stall. As the stall progressed, the aircraft lost lift and began to descend uncontrollably. The pilots, recognizing the severity of the situation, ejected from the aircraft just before it crashed, narrowly escaping with their lives. The B-2 impacted the ground, resulting in a massive explosion and the total loss of the aircraft.

The crash site was immediately secured, and an investigation was launched to determine the cause of the accident. The Air Force Accident Investigation Board (AIB) conducted a thorough review of the events leading up to the crash, examining the aircraft's maintenance records, sensor data, and the environmental conditions on the day of the accident. The investigation revealed that the primary cause of the crash was the failure of the Air Data System sensors, which had been contaminated by moisture.

The report highlighted several contributing factors. First, the procedures for maintaining and checking the sensor heaters were found to be inadequate. The heaters, which were designed to prevent moisture accumulation, were not activated, leading to the failure of the sensors to provide accurate data. Additionally, the pre-flight checks did not detect the sensor failure, and the reliance on automated systems to interpret and act on the erroneous data without adequate human oversight compounded the problem.

The findings from the investigation prompted immediate changes in the maintenance and operational procedures for the B-2 fleet. The Air Force implemented more rigorous checks for the Air Data System and other critical sensors, ensuring that they were free from moisture and functioning correctly before each flight. Training programs were updated to emphasize the importance of understanding and verifying sensor data, even in highly automated systems, to prevent similar incidents in the future.

The crash also underscored the vulnerabilities of advanced technology in military aviation. While the B-2 Spirit is an engineering marvel, the incident revealed that even the most sophisticated systems can fail if basic maintenance and operational protocols are not followed. The lessons learned from this crash extended beyond the B-2 program, influencing maintenance and operational standards across various platforms in the U.S. Air Force and prompting a reevaluation of the balance between automation and human oversight in flight operations.

In the broader context, the crash raised important questions about the cost and complexity of maintaining advanced military assets. The loss of a single B-2 represented a significant financial setback, highlighting the challenges associated with operating and sustaining a fleet of such advanced and expensive aircraft. This incident, coupled with other maintenance and operational challenges faced by high-tech military platforms, spurred discussions about the future of stealth and other advanced technologies in military aviation.

Moreover, the crash had implications for the strategic capabilities of the U.S. Air Force. The B-2 Spirit, with its ability to deliver precision strikes over long distances while evading detection, is a key component of the United States' deterrence and power projection capabilities. The loss of an aircraft not only reduced the available fleet but also necessitated a review of how such critical assets are deployed and maintained to ensure their readiness and reliability.

The B-2 bomber crash due to sensor failure thus stands as a significant event in military aviation history. It serves as a stark reminder of the importance of rigorous maintenance practices, the need for effective human oversight of automated systems, and the challenges associated with operating and sustaining advanced military technology. The lessons learned from this incident continue to inform and shape the practices and policies of the U.S. Air Force, ensuring that the tragic loss of the "Spirit of Kansas" contributes to the enhancement of safety and reliability in military aviation.

Chapter 32: The Love Canal Toxic Waste Dump

The Love Canal toxic waste dump is a profound example of environmental negligence and its disastrous impact on a community. Located in Niagara Falls, New York, Love Canal became synonymous with hazardous waste mismanagement, leading to severe health crises and a landmark environmental movement in the United States.

The story of Love Canal begins in the early 20th century when William T. Love, an ambitious entrepreneur, envisioned constructing a model industrial city powered by hydroelectric energy from a canal that would bypass Niagara Falls. His dream was to create a utopian community with affordable energy. However, due to financial difficulties and changing economic conditions, Love's vision never fully materialized. By 1910, the canal project was abandoned, leaving a partially dug trench about 16 acres in size.

In the following decades, the canal site became a dumping ground for industrial waste. The Hooker Chemical Company, which later became a subsidiary of Occidental Petroleum, acquired the site in the 1940s and began using it as a disposal area for chemical waste. From 1942 to 1953, Hooker Chemical dumped approximately 21,000 tons of toxic chemicals into the canal, including substances like dioxin, benzene, and other carcinogens. The waste was buried in metal drums and sealed with clay to prevent leakage, but the site was far from secure.

In 1953, Hooker Chemical, realizing the potential liability of the waste site, sold the land to the Niagara Falls School Board for one dollar. The deed transfer included a warning about the chemical waste buried on the site, but it did not deter development. The school board, disregarding the risks, constructed a school and a residential neighborhood on and around the former dump site. Over time, about

800 single-family homes and 240 low-income apartments were built, housing approximately 1,000 families.

For years, residents of Love Canal lived unknowingly atop a toxic waste dump. By the 1970s, however, alarming signs of environmental and health issues began to surface. Residents reported foul odors, chemical residues seeping into their basements, and puddles of noxious substances appearing in their yards. Children suffered burns from playing on contaminated soil, and the community experienced an unusually high rate of illnesses, including epilepsy, asthma, and miscarriages. Cancer cases also appeared to be abnormally frequent.

The turning point came in 1978 when investigative journalism and grassroots activism brought national attention to the crisis at Love Canal. Lois Gibbs, a local resident and mother, became a leading figure in the fight for justice. She organized the Love Canal Homeowners Association, which conducted door-to-door surveys revealing the extent of health problems in the community. Gibbs and other activists demanded action from local, state, and federal authorities.

In response to mounting public pressure, New York State and the federal government initiated investigations into the environmental contamination at Love Canal. The findings were shocking: toxic chemicals had migrated from the canal site, contaminating the soil and groundwater throughout the neighborhood. The situation was declared a public health emergency, and in August 1978, President Jimmy Carter authorized federal funds to relocate the most affected families. Over 200 families were evacuated immediately, and eventually, over 800 families were relocated from the area.

The Love Canal disaster had far-reaching consequences. It prompted significant changes in environmental policy and regulation in the United States. In 1980, Congress enacted the Comprehensive Environmental Response, Compensation, and Liability Act (CERCLA), commonly known as the Superfund Act. This landmark legislation provided the federal government with the authority and funds to clean up hazardous waste sites and hold polluters accountable for environmental damage. The Superfund program has since been used to address thousands of contaminated sites across the country.

The cleanup of Love Canal itself was an extensive and expensive effort. The Environmental Protection Agency (EPA) oversaw the remediation process, which included the excavation and removal of contaminated soil, the installation of a drainage system to contain and treat leachate, and the capping of the landfill with an impermeable barrier. The site was eventually declared safe for limited use, although many former residents continued to suffer from health issues and sought compensation through legal channels.

The legacy of Love Canal extends beyond environmental policy and remediation. It galvanized the environmental movement in the United States, raising public awareness about the dangers of industrial pollution and the need for stringent environmental protections. The disaster highlighted the importance of community activism and the role of ordinary citizens in holding corporations and governments accountable for environmental harm.

Lois Gibbs' advocacy did not end with Love Canal. She founded the Center for Health, Environment, and Justice (CHEJ), an organization dedicated to helping communities facing environmental threats. Through CHEJ, Gibbs has supported grassroots efforts to address environmental injustices across the country, empowering communities to fight for their health and safety.

The Love Canal incident also underscored the need for better land use planning and the importance of considering environmental history in development decisions. The failure to heed the warnings about the chemical waste buried at Love Canal and the subsequent development of homes and a school on the site exemplify the consequences of neglecting environmental risks. This case has served as a cautionary tale for urban planners, developers, and policymakers, emphasizing the need for comprehensive environmental assessments before undertaking construction projects.

Furthermore, the Love Canal disaster highlighted the inadequacies in regulatory oversight and corporate responsibility at the time. Hooker Chemical's decision to sell the contaminated land without ensuring proper cleanup measures and the lack of effective government intervention until the crisis reached a tipping point demonstrated significant gaps in environmental governance. The incident led to a reevaluation of corporate practices and regulatory frameworks, pushing for greater transparency, accountability, and preventive measures to avoid similar catastrophes in the future.

The human impact of the Love Canal disaster is profound. Many former residents continue to live with the health consequences of exposure to toxic chemicals. The psychological toll of displacement, illness, and the fight for justice has left lasting scars on the community. The Love Canal tragedy serves as a powerful reminder of the enduring effects of environmental negligence on individuals and families.

Chapter 33: The Great Smog of London 1952

The Great Smog of London in 1952 stands as one of the most severe air pollution events in the history of the United Kingdom and the world. This environmental disaster brought London to a near standstill and had catastrophic effects on the health of its residents, leading to widespread illness and a significant death toll. The event not only highlighted the dangers of industrial pollution but also served as a catalyst for significant changes in environmental policies and regulations.

The Great Smog occurred between December 5 and December 9, 1952, when a period of unusually cold weather combined with an anticyclone and windless conditions to create a dense layer of smog that blanketed the city of London. The immediate cause of the smog was the burning of large quantities of coal, both in homes for heating and in factories for industrial processes. At the time, coal was the primary source of energy in London, and the type of coal being used was often of poor quality, producing higher levels of sulfur dioxide and particulate matter when burned.

As the cold weather set in, residents increased their use of coal fires to keep warm, resulting in a significant rise in airborne pollutants. Normally, such pollutants would be dispersed by the wind, but the atmospheric conditions during that week in December trapped the polluted air close to the ground. This phenomenon is known as a temperature inversion, where a layer of warm air sits above cooler air near the ground, preventing the cooler air—and the pollutants within it—from rising and dispersing.

The smog that formed was a thick, yellowish-brown fog that reduced visibility to just a few meters. It infiltrated homes, businesses, and public buildings, creating an almost unbearable environment for the city's inhabitants. Transportation was severely disrupted, with road, rail, and air travel coming to a virtual halt. Buses and cars crawled through the streets at a snail's pace, often with conductors walking in front of them to guide the way. The lack of visibility caused numerous accidents, and the city's ambulance service struggled to respond to emergencies.

The health impact of the Great Smog was immediate and devastating. The dense smog was laden with sulfur dioxide, carbon monoxide, and particulate matter, which caused severe respiratory problems. Hospitals were overwhelmed with patients suffering from breathing difficulties, and doctors reported a dramatic increase in cases of bronchitis, pneumonia, and other respiratory ailments. The very young, the elderly, and those with pre-existing health conditions were particularly vulnerable.

The official death toll attributed to the Great Smog was initially reported as around 4,000 people, but later research has suggested that the number was likely much higher. Studies conducted in the years following the event estimated that the smog may have caused as many as 12,000 deaths, with thousands more suffering long-term health effects. The smog's impact extended beyond immediate respiratory problems, contributing to cardiovascular issues and exacerbating chronic illnesses.

In the aftermath of the disaster, public outrage and the demand for action grew. The severity of the Great Smog exposed the urgent need for improved air quality and stricter controls on industrial emissions. The event spurred the British government to take measures to address air pollution, leading to significant changes in environmental policy.

One of the most important outcomes was the passage of the Clean Air Act of 1956. This landmark legislation aimed to reduce air pollution by controlling the types of fuel that could be burned in urban areas. The act introduced "smoke control areas" where only smokeless fuels could be used, effectively banning the use of coal that produced high levels of smoke and sulfur dioxide. The Clean Air Act also provided for the relocation of power stations away from urban areas and encouraged the use of cleaner fuels and technologies.

The Clean Air Act of 1956 was a pivotal moment in the history of environmental regulation, setting a precedent for future legislation aimed at reducing air pollution and protecting public health. It marked the beginning of a shift towards greater environmental awareness and responsibility, not only in the United Kingdom but also around the world.

The Great Smog of London also had a profound impact on scientific research and the understanding of air pollution. The event prompted extensive studies into the sources, composition, and effects of air pollutants. Scientists and health experts investigated the relationship between air quality and health, leading to a deeper understanding of the dangers posed by airborne contaminants. This research laid the groundwork for future advancements in environmental science and public health.

The legacy of the Great Smog is evident in the continued efforts to improve air quality and reduce pollution. In the decades following the disaster, additional measures were taken to address air pollution, including the introduction of stricter emissions standards for vehicles and industrial facilities. Advances in technology and changes in energy sources have further contributed to cleaner air in London and other cities.

Despite these improvements, the lessons of the Great Smog remain relevant today. Air pollution continues to be a major environmental and public health issue globally, with millions of people affected by poor air quality each year. The event serves as a stark reminder of the importance of robust environmental policies, the need for continued vigilance in monitoring air quality, and the necessity of sustainable practices to protect the health and well-being of populations.

In recent years, the issue of air pollution has gained renewed attention as cities around the world grapple with smog and its health impacts. The rise of industrialization, increased vehicular traffic, and the burning of fossil fuels continue to contribute to air pollution, prompting governments and organizations to seek solutions to this persistent problem. The experiences and lessons learned from the Great Smog of London provide valuable insights for contemporary efforts to combat air pollution and improve environmental health.

Chapter 34: The Great Fire of London 1666

The Great Fire of London in 1666 is one of the most infamous events in the history of England's capital. It was a devastating conflagration that swept through the central parts of London from Sunday, September 2, to Thursday, September 6, destroying a large portion of the city and leaving a lasting impact on its architecture and urban development. This disaster not only reshaped the physical landscape of London but also had profound social and economic consequences, influencing building regulations and firefighting techniques for centuries to come.

The fire began in a small bakery on Pudding Lane owned by Thomas Farriner, the King's baker. In the early hours of Sunday morning, a spark from the bakery's oven ignited the wooden building. The summer of 1666 had been exceptionally dry, and a strong easterly wind fanned the flames, quickly spreading the fire to neighboring houses. The buildings in London at that time were predominantly made of timber and thatched roofs, which were highly flammable. Additionally, the houses were built very close together, with narrow, winding streets that facilitated the rapid spread of the fire.

The initial response to the fire was chaotic. The Lord Mayor of London, Sir Thomas Bloodworth, underestimated the severity of the situation, famously dismissing it as a minor issue that could be extinguished with ease. This delay in ordering decisive action allowed the fire to gain momentum. As the flames spread, panicked residents fled their homes, trying to save whatever possessions they could carry. Many people sought refuge in open spaces such as Moorfields and Finsbury Fields, while others crossed the River Thames to Southwark.

By Monday, the fire had engulfed much of the medieval city. The dense network of wooden buildings acted as tinder, and the strong winds continued to drive the fire westward. Key structures, including St. Paul's Cathedral, were consumed by the flames. The old St. Paul's Cathedral was a massive structure with a wooden roof, and the intense heat caused its lead roof to melt, running down the streets like a river of molten metal. The cathedral's destruction was a significant cultural and religious loss for the city.

Firefighting efforts during the Great Fire were hampered by several factors. The technology and techniques available at the time were rudimentary. The primary method of firefighting involved creating firebreaks by demolishing buildings in the path of the flames to stop the fire from spreading further. However, this method was implemented too late, and the strong winds often carried embers across the firebreaks, igniting new fires. Fire hooks, buckets of water, and primitive fire engines were used, but they were largely ineffective against the rapidly spreading blaze.

King Charles II took a personal interest in the firefighting efforts and ordered the use of gunpowder to create more effective firebreaks. Soldiers were deployed to demolish buildings, and although this measure was more successful, it came after much of the damage had already been done. The use of gunpowder was dangerous and added to the chaos and destruction, but it ultimately helped to halt the westward spread of the fire.

By Tuesday, the fire had reached its peak, and the easterly winds began to die down, which helped to slow the spread of the flames. On Wednesday, the fire started to burn itself out, having consumed the majority of the city's combustible materials. By Thursday, the fire was largely under control, although isolated pockets continued to smolder for several more days.

The aftermath of the Great Fire of London was catastrophic. It is estimated that the fire destroyed 87 parish churches, 13,200 houses, 52 Livery Company halls, numerous civic buildings including the Royal Exchange, the Guildhall, and a variety of shops, inns, and taverns.

Approximately 80,000 people, roughly one-sixth of London's population at the time, were left homeless. Miraculously, the official death toll was recorded as relatively low, with only a handful of confirmed fatalities. However, it is likely that many more people, particularly the poor and those whose deaths went unrecorded, perished in the flames or from subsequent exposure and disease.

The economic impact of the fire was immense. The destruction of homes and businesses led to a significant financial burden for the survivors, many of whom lost everything. The rebuilding of London required a massive effort and substantial resources. King Charles II and his government faced the enormous challenge of reconstructing the city while also addressing the needs of the displaced population.

In the wake of the fire, a variety of measures were introduced to prevent such a disaster from occurring again. Rebuilding efforts were guided by a series of regulations aimed at making the new London more fire-resistant. The Rebuilding Act of 1667 mandated the use of brick and stone for new constructions, rather than the easily combustible timber that had fueled the fire. Streets were widened, and building regulations were established to ensure greater spacing between structures. These measures aimed to reduce the risk of fire spreading rapidly through densely packed buildings.

One of the most notable outcomes of the rebuilding effort was the architectural transformation of London. Sir Christopher Wren, one of the leading architects of the time, played a pivotal role in the reconstruction. Wren designed several new churches, including the magnificent St. Paul's Cathedral, which became a symbol of the city's resilience and renewal. The new St. Paul's was constructed with a grand dome and an imposing façade, representing a departure from the Gothic style of the old cathedral and embracing the classical influences of the Renaissance.

The Great Fire also had a profound impact on urban planning and public health. The rebuilding efforts included improvements to the city's infrastructure, such as better drainage systems and wider streets, which helped to reduce the spread of diseases. The fire effectively eradicated the remnants of the plague that had ravaged London just a year earlier, as the flames destroyed many of the unsanitary conditions that had contributed to the epidemic.

In addition to the physical reconstruction, the Great Fire of London had significant social and cultural ramifications. The disaster prompted a re-evaluation of fire safety practices and the establishment of more organized firefighting services. The insurance industry also evolved in response to the fire, with the creation of fire insurance companies that offered coverage to property owners, providing financial protection against future fires.

The legacy of the Great Fire of London extends beyond its immediate aftermath. The event has been immortalized in literature, art, and popular culture, serving as a powerful reminder of the vulnerability of urban centers to natural and man-made disasters. It has also been the subject of extensive historical research, with scholars examining the causes, effects, and responses to the fire to gain insights into urban resilience and disaster management.

Chapter 35: The Peshtigo Firestorm Ignition

The Peshtigo Firestorm of 1871 is one of the most devastating and lesser-known natural disasters in American history. Occurring on the same day as the Great Chicago Fire, the Peshtigo Firestorm swept through northeastern Wisconsin, annihilating everything in its path and causing a staggering loss of life. The fire was the deadliest in U.S. history, yet its story has been overshadowed by the concurrent blaze in Chicago. The Peshtigo Firestorm's origins, progression, and aftermath provide a harrowing account of nature's fury and human resilience.

The Peshtigo Firestorm ignited on October 8, 1871, in the town of Peshtigo, Wisconsin, situated along the Peshtigo River. Several factors contributed to the catastrophic fire conditions. The summer and early autumn of 1871 had been exceptionally dry, creating a tinderbox in the forests surrounding Peshtigo. Logging operations in the area, a common industry at the time, left vast amounts of slash—piles of dry branches, bark, and other debris—scattered across the forest floor. Additionally, agricultural practices included clearing land using controlled burns, which often went unchecked.

These dry conditions, combined with strong winds and the abundant dry fuel, set the stage for disaster. On the evening of October 8, a cold front moved into the area, bringing with it powerful winds that reached gale force. These winds fanned small, scattered fires into a massive inferno that would come to be known as the Peshtigo Firestorm. The blaze rapidly grew in intensity, creating a firestorm—a phenomenon where the fire becomes so large and intense that it creates its own weather system, including tornadoes of fire and hurricane-force winds.

The firestorm moved with terrifying speed, engulfing the town of Peshtigo and surrounding areas. Witnesses described a wall of flame advancing at a pace too fast to outrun. The heat was so intense that it melted sand into glass and caused the waters of the Peshtigo River to boil. People seeking refuge in the river found themselves scalded by the superheated water. The firestorm produced whirlwinds of flame, known as fire whirls or fire tornadoes, which lifted people, animals, and debris into the air, adding to the chaos and destruction.

In the face of such an unstoppable force, many residents had little time to react. Some fled to the river, hoping the water would provide shelter from the flames, while others sought refuge in wells, cellars, or open fields. However, these attempts were often futile against the intensity of the firestorm. The extreme heat and lack of breathable air claimed many lives, with people succumbing to burns, smoke inhalation, or drowning in their desperate attempts to escape.

The town of Peshtigo was completely destroyed, along with several other communities in the region. The firestorm consumed an estimated 1.2 million acres of land, leaving a charred landscape in its wake. The exact death toll is unknown, but it is estimated that between 1,200 and 2,500 people perished in the blaze. Many of the bodies were so badly burned that they could not be identified, and mass graves were used to bury the dead.

The aftermath of the Peshtigo Firestorm was marked by devastation and despair. Survivors emerged to find their homes, farms, and towns reduced to ashes. The economic impact was severe, as the region's primary industries—logging and agriculture—were decimated. Relief efforts were hampered by the simultaneous occurrence of the Great Chicago Fire, which diverted national attention and resources away from Peshtigo.

In the days and weeks following the fire, relief committees were formed to provide aid to the survivors. The state of Wisconsin and neighboring states sent food, clothing, and other supplies to the affected areas. The federal government also provided assistance, but the scale of the disaster made recovery a slow and challenging process.

Many survivors were left homeless and destitute, struggling to rebuild their lives from the ashes.

The Peshtigo Firestorm prompted changes in forestry and land management practices. The disaster highlighted the dangers of unchecked land clearing and the accumulation of dry fuel in forested areas. In response, new regulations and practices were implemented to reduce the risk of similar fires. These included controlled burns, better management of logging debris, and the establishment of firebreaks to help contain future blazes.

The legacy of the Peshtigo Firestorm extends beyond the immediate aftermath and changes in land management. The disaster has been studied by historians, scientists, and fire management professionals to understand the conditions that led to the firestorm and to develop strategies for preventing and responding to similar events. The story of the Peshtigo Firestorm serves as a sobering reminder of the power of nature and the importance of preparedness and resilience in the face of disaster.

In the years since the fire, the town of Peshtigo has commemorated the event with memorials and a museum dedicated to preserving the history of the fire and honoring the memory of those who perished. The Peshtigo Fire Museum houses artifacts, photographs, and accounts from survivors, providing visitors with a poignant and educational experience.

The Peshtigo Firestorm also offers important lessons for contemporary fire management and disaster preparedness. As wildfires continue to pose a significant threat in many parts of the world, the experiences of Peshtigo underscore the need for effective fire prevention and response strategies. These include proper forest management, early warning systems, and community preparedness plans to help mitigate the impact of wildfires and protect lives and property.

Chapter 36: The Hillsborough Stadium Crush

The Hillsborough Stadium disaster remains one of the most tragic and significant events in the history of British sports, symbolizing not only a catastrophic failure of crowd management but also a profound miscarriage of justice that spanned decades. The disaster occurred on April 15, 1989, during an FA Cup semi-final match between Liverpool and Nottingham Forest at Hillsborough Stadium in Sheffield, England. It resulted in the deaths of 96 Liverpool fans and injuries to hundreds more, marking it as the worst disaster in British sporting history. The ramifications of this tragedy extend far beyond the event itself, highlighting critical issues in stadium safety, police accountability, media ethics, and the quest for justice by bereaved families.

The root causes of the Hillsborough disaster lay in several factors, including inadequate stadium design, poor crowd management, and a lack of effective emergency response procedures. Hillsborough Stadium was chosen as the venue for the semi-final due to its capacity and central location. However, the stadium had a history of safety issues and previous incidents of overcrowding. The Leppings Lane end of the stadium, where the disaster occurred, was particularly problematic. This area consisted of a series of terraces separated by metal fences, creating pens that were intended to control the movement of fans. However, these fences ultimately trapped fans in the deadly crush.

On the day of the match, a series of critical errors and misjudgments by the South Yorkshire Police exacerbated the situation. Due to delays caused by traffic and overcrowded turnstiles, a large number of Liverpool fans were still outside the stadium as the match was about to begin. To alleviate the congestion outside, Chief

Superintendent David Duckenfield, the police officer in charge, ordered the opening of an exit gate (Gate C), which allowed thousands of fans to surge into the already overcrowded central pens behind the goal. This decision was made without ensuring that the flow of people into the pens could be controlled or monitored.

As fans continued to pour into the pens, the pressure became unbearable. Those at the front were pressed against the perimeter fences, unable to escape the crush. The situation quickly escalated into a catastrophic crowd crush, with fans desperately trying to climb over barriers and fences to escape. Despite the obvious signs of distress, the match continued for several minutes before being halted. The police, stewards, and emergency services were slow to react, and their efforts were hampered by the confusion and chaos.

In the aftermath of the disaster, the initial response from the authorities and the media compounded the tragedy. The South Yorkshire Police and certain sections of the media, notably The Sun newspaper, sought to shift the blame onto the fans themselves. The Sun's infamous front-page headline, "The Truth," falsely accused Liverpool fans of drunkenness, ticketless entry, and even theft from the dead. These baseless accusations caused immense pain and outrage among the grieving families and the wider Liverpool community.

The official inquiry into the disaster, led by Lord Justice Taylor, concluded in 1990 with the publication of the Taylor Report. The report exonerated the fans of any wrongdoing and placed the blame squarely on the shoulders of the police and the stadium's design. It highlighted the failures in crowd control, inadequate safety measures, and the lack of proper emergency response. The Taylor Report led to significant changes in British football, including the introduction of all-seater stadiums and improved safety standards. However, for many of the bereaved families and survivors, the fight for justice was far from over.

For over two decades, the families of the victims campaigned tirelessly for a full investigation and accountability for those responsible. Their persistence led to the establishment of the Hillsborough Independent Panel in 2009, which reviewed previously unseen documents and evidence related to the disaster. The panel's findings, published in 2012, revealed shocking details of a cover-up orchestrated by the South Yorkshire Police. It was revealed that police statements had been altered to remove any criticism of their actions, and a systematic effort had been made to deflect blame onto the fans.

The revelations of the Hillsborough Independent Panel prompted a new inquest into the disaster, which began in 2014 and concluded in 2016. The inquest jury returned a verdict of unlawful killing, determining that the actions of the police and emergency services contributed significantly to the deaths of the 96 fans. The verdict was a momentous victory for the families and supporters, who had long sought recognition of the true causes of the disaster.

The implications of the Hillsborough disaster extended beyond the immediate changes in stadium safety and crowd management. It exposed deep flaws in the British justice system, the accountability of public institutions, and the role of the media in shaping public perception. The disaster also highlighted the resilience and determination of the victims' families, who faced years of adversity in their quest for truth and justice. Their efforts have been instrumental in fostering a greater awareness of the need for transparency and accountability in the aftermath of public tragedies.

In terms of legacy, the Hillsborough disaster has had a profound impact on British football and society. The introduction of all-seater stadiums and stricter safety regulations have significantly improved the safety of football matches, reducing the likelihood of similar tragedies occurring. The disaster also led to reforms in the way public institutions handle disasters and their aftermath, with an emphasis on transparency and accountability.

Moreover, the Hillsborough disaster has left an indelible mark on the collective memory of Liverpool and the wider football community. Annual memorial services are held at Anfield, Liverpool's home ground, to honor the memory of the 96 fans who lost their lives. The phrase "You'll Never Walk Alone," a Liverpool anthem, has come to symbolize the solidarity and support of the Liverpool community in the face of adversity.

Chapter 37: The Aberfan Coal Slurry Disaster

The Aberfan coal slurry disaster, one of the most tragic events in Welsh history, occurred on October 21, 1966, in the village of Aberfan, located in South Wales. This catastrophic event resulted in the deaths of 144 people, including 116 children, when a colliery spoil tip collapsed, engulfing Pantglas Junior School and nearby houses. The disaster highlighted the fatal consequences of industrial negligence, the failure of regulatory oversight, and the profound human cost of coal mining in Britain. The Aberfan disaster's origins, immediate impact, and long-term ramifications continue to resonate as a sobering reminder of the importance of safety and accountability in industrial practices.

Aberfan, a small mining village, was surrounded by several colliery spoil tips—large mounds of waste material extracted from coal mines. These tips were composed of loose rock, shale, and other byproducts of mining, often piled high and precariously on hillsides. Tip No. 7, the one that collapsed, was situated directly above the village, on a mountainside known as Merthyr Mountain. The tip was approximately 111 feet high and had been built on a stream, an unstable foundation that contributed to its eventual collapse.

In the years leading up to the disaster, there had been numerous warnings about the stability of the spoil tips. Residents and miners had reported several small slides and instances of water emerging from the tips, indicating potential instability. However, these warnings were largely ignored by the National Coal Board (NCB), the organization responsible for managing coal mines and their waste. The NCB assured the public that the tips were safe, despite growing evidence to the contrary.

On the morning of October 21, 1966, after days of heavy rain, the accumulated water within Tip No. 7 caused it to become saturated and unstable. At around 9:15 AM, the tip suddenly gave way, sending approximately 140,000 cubic yards of slurry, consisting of coal waste and water, hurtling down the mountainside. The massive wave of slurry traveled at high speed, demolishing everything in its path. It first struck Pantglas Junior School, where the children had just begun their lessons, and then engulfed nearby homes.

The impact on Pantglas Junior School was catastrophic. The slurry smashed through the walls and windows, filling classrooms and trapping children and teachers inside. Many were unable to escape the torrent of mud and debris. The noise of the collapse and the subsequent chaos could be heard throughout the village, drawing residents to the scene in a desperate attempt to rescue survivors. Parents, miners, and emergency responders worked frantically, using their bare hands and makeshift tools to dig through the slurry and rubble in search of their loved ones.

The immediate aftermath of the disaster was marked by scenes of unimaginable grief and devastation. The village of Aberfan was left in shock as the extent of the tragedy became clear. Rescuers toiled day and night, but hopes of finding survivors dwindled as time passed. By the end of the rescue operation, 144 people had been confirmed dead, including 116 children, most of whom were between the ages of seven and ten. The loss of so many young lives devastated the close-knit community and left a lasting scar on the village.

In the wake of the disaster, an official inquiry was launched to investigate the causes and assign responsibility. The inquiry, led by Lord Justice Edmund Davies, found that the NCB was primarily responsible for the disaster. The report criticized the NCB for its failure to heed warnings about the instability of the spoil tips and for its negligent management practices. The inquiry revealed that the tips had been constructed without proper consideration of geological conditions, and the decision to place Tip No. 7 on a stream had been particularly reckless.

The inquiry's findings were damning, yet despite the clear evidence of negligence, no individuals within the NCB were held criminally accountable for the disaster. The NCB and its chairman, Lord Robens, issued apologies and expressed regret, but the affected families and the wider public felt that justice had not been served. The compensation offered to the victims' families was seen as inadequate, adding to the sense of injustice.

The Aberfan disaster had significant long-term implications for mining practices and industrial safety in the United Kingdom. It led to changes in the management and regulation of colliery spoil tips, including stricter safety standards and more rigorous inspections. The NCB was eventually dissolved in 1987, and its responsibilities were transferred to other organizations. The disaster also contributed to a broader recognition of the need for corporate accountability and the protection of communities from industrial hazards.

In addition to regulatory changes, the disaster had a profound social and psychological impact on the village of Aberfan. The loss of so many children and the trauma experienced by survivors left deep emotional scars. Memorial services and commemorations became an integral part of the community's efforts to cope with the tragedy. In the years following the disaster, a memorial garden was established on the site of Pantglas Junior School, serving as a place of reflection and remembrance for those who lost their lives.

The story of Aberfan also inspired various forms of artistic and cultural expression, helping to keep the memory of the disaster alive. Books, documentaries, and films have been produced, recounting the events and honoring the resilience of the Aberfan community. One of the most poignant representations is the memorial hymn "Aberfan," which captures the sorrow and the enduring spirit of the village.

The legacy of Aberfan extends beyond the immediate community. The disaster serves as a powerful reminder of the human cost of industrial negligence and the importance of ensuring the safety and well-being of workers and communities affected by industrial activities. It underscores the need for vigilance, accountability, and compassion in the management of industrial operations and the protection of vulnerable populations.

Chapter 38: The Texas City Disaster of 1947

The Texas City Disaster of 1947 stands as one of the most devastating industrial accidents in U.S. history. Occurring on April 16, 1947, in the Port of Texas City, Texas, this catastrophe was triggered by a fire on board the SS Grandcamp, a French-registered vessel carrying a large quantity of ammonium nitrate fertilizer. The ensuing explosions killed nearly 600 people, injured thousands, and caused widespread destruction. The disaster highlighted the potential dangers of industrial chemicals, spurred changes in regulations and safety standards, and remains a sobering reminder of the potential for large-scale industrial catastrophes.

Texas City, located on the Gulf of Mexico near Galveston, was a burgeoning industrial hub in the mid-20th century. Its port was a crucial node in the distribution of goods, particularly chemicals and petroleum products. The SS Grandcamp arrived at Texas City on April 11, 1947, with a cargo that included 2,300 tons of ammonium nitrate, a compound widely used as a fertilizer but also highly explosive under certain conditions. The ammonium nitrate on the Grandcamp was packaged in paper sacks, a common practice at the time, and stored in the ship's hold.

On the morning of April 16, longshoremen loading cargo onto the Grandcamp noticed smoke coming from the hold. Despite attempts to extinguish the fire with water, the crew switched to steam, hoping to smother the flames and save the cargo from water damage. This decision proved to be critical, as the steam did not effectively suppress the fire, which continued to smolder and increase in temperature. Ammonium nitrate, when exposed to high heat, undergoes a chemical reaction that can lead to detonation, particularly if confined and allowed to reach a critical temperature.

As the fire grew, a large crowd of spectators gathered, drawn by the thick smoke billowing from the ship. The ship's crew and port authorities were unaware of the imminent danger posed by the chemical reaction taking place within the hold. At approximately 9:12 AM, the ammonium nitrate reached its explosive threshold. The resulting detonation was catastrophic: the explosion obliterated the Grandcamp and generated a massive blast wave, felt as far as 100 miles away. The explosion released an estimated 2.7 kilotons of energy, equivalent to a small nuclear bomb.

The immediate aftermath was sheer chaos. The explosion caused a massive fireball that ignited nearby structures, oil refineries, and other vessels docked at the port. The blast created a 15-foot tidal wave, which further spread the fires and caused additional damage. Hundreds of buildings were destroyed or heavily damaged, including homes, businesses, and industrial facilities. Windows were shattered in Galveston, 10 miles away, and the shock wave was detected as far as Louisiana.

The human toll was staggering. Nearly 600 people lost their lives, including the entire Texas City Volunteer Fire Department, which had been attempting to control the fire on the Grandcamp. The exact number of fatalities remains uncertain due to the intensity of the blast and the widespread destruction. Thousands more were injured, many suffering severe burns, lacerations, and other traumatic injuries. Hospitals in Texas City and surrounding areas were overwhelmed by the influx of casualties, and emergency responders struggled to cope with the scale of the disaster.

Adding to the horror, the devastation was not confined to a single explosion. On the following day, April 17, a second explosion occurred when the SS High Flyer, another ship loaded with ammonium nitrate and sulfur, detonated. The High Flyer had been damaged and set ablaze by the initial blast but was not evacuated or moved in time to prevent the second catastrophe. This explosion caused additional deaths, injuries, and destruction, further compounding the disaster's impact.

The Texas City Disaster prompted immediate and long-term responses from various sectors. In the short term, emergency relief efforts were mobilized to provide medical care, shelter, and support for the survivors. The Red Cross, military units, and neighboring communities played crucial roles in the relief operations. Temporary morgues were established to handle the large number of fatalities, and search and rescue efforts continued for days as authorities combed through the rubble for survivors and victims.

In the wake of the disaster, investigations were launched to determine the causes and identify measures to prevent similar occurrences. The primary cause was quickly identified as the ignition and detonation of the ammonium nitrate cargo. The exact source of the initial fire remains unknown, but it is believed to have been accidental, possibly caused by a discarded cigarette or faulty equipment. The investigation also highlighted the lack of awareness and preparedness for handling such volatile substances, both among the ship's crew and port authorities.

The disaster led to significant changes in the regulation and handling of hazardous materials. The U.S. government and various regulatory bodies introduced stricter controls and guidelines for the storage, transportation, and handling of chemicals like ammonium nitrate. The Occupational Safety and Health Administration (OSHA) and other agencies developed comprehensive safety standards to mitigate the risks associated with industrial chemicals. These regulations included improved labeling, storage requirements, and emergency response protocols.

The Texas City Disaster also had profound legal and financial repercussions. A series of lawsuits were filed against the government and companies involved in the shipment and handling of the ammonium nitrate. The lawsuits culminated in the landmark Supreme

Court case Dalehite v. United States (1953), which addressed the extent of government liability in such incidents. The court ultimately ruled that the government could not be held liable under the Federal Tort Claims Act, citing the discretionary function exception. This decision underscored the complexities of legal accountability in large-scale industrial accidents.

Economically, the disaster had a severe impact on Texas City and its residents. The destruction of industrial facilities, businesses, and homes caused significant financial losses and disrupted the local economy. Rebuilding efforts took years, and many families and businesses faced immense challenges in recovering from the devastation. However, the community demonstrated remarkable resilience, coming together to rebuild and support one another in the aftermath of the tragedy.

The legacy of the Texas City Disaster extends beyond regulatory changes and economic impacts. It served as a poignant reminder of the potential dangers inherent in industrial activities and the need for constant vigilance and preparedness. The disaster highlighted the importance of safety training, effective emergency response plans, and the proper handling of hazardous materials. It also underscored the necessity of community awareness and engagement in industrial safety practices.

Memorials and commemorations have been established to honor the victims and survivors of the Texas City Disaster. These include monuments, plaques, and annual ceremonies that serve as reminders of the lives lost and the enduring impact of the event on the community. The disaster is also remembered through historical documentation, educational programs, and exhibitions that aim to preserve the memory of the event and its lessons for future generations.

Chapter 39: The Boston Marathon Bombing Misstep

The Boston Marathon bombing on April 15, 2013, is a grim reminder of the devastating impacts of terrorism on public safety and the importance of meticulous intelligence and security measures. The bombing, carried out by brothers Tamerlan and Dzhokhar Tsarnaev, not only resulted in significant loss of life and injury but also exposed critical lapses in law enforcement and intelligence-sharing processes that could have potentially prevented the attack or mitigated its impact. Understanding the detailed events, aftermath, and lessons learned from this incident is essential to improving counterterrorism strategies and ensuring public safety in large-scale events.

The Boston Marathon is an annual event held on Patriots' Day, attracting thousands of runners and spectators from around the world. On April 15, 2013, as runners were approaching the finish line, two homemade pressure cooker bombs detonated 12 seconds and 210 yards apart near the race's end point on Boylston Street. The bombs killed three people—29-year-old Krystle Campbell, 8-year-old Martin Richard, and 23-year-old Lingzi Lu—and injured over 260 others, causing horrific injuries including traumatic amputations, burns, and shrapnel wounds. The bombs, filled with nails, ball bearings, and other shrapnel, were designed to maximize harm to those in the vicinity.

The immediate aftermath of the bombing saw a massive response from emergency services. First responders, including police, firefighters, and medical personnel, acted swiftly to tend to the wounded and secure the area. The injured were transported to nearby hospitals, some in critical condition. The Boston medical community, with its extensive network of hospitals and trauma centers, played a crucial role in treating the victims, preventing further loss of life despite the severity of many injuries.

Law enforcement agencies launched a massive manhunt for the perpetrators. The Federal Bureau of Investigation (FBI), Boston Police Department, Massachusetts State Police, and other agencies worked together to investigate the incident. The FBI released photographs and surveillance footage of two suspects—later identified as the Tsarnaev brothers—on April 18, asking the public for assistance in identifying them. The release of these images was a critical turning point in the investigation, as tips from the public helped law enforcement narrow their search.

The Tsarnaev brothers' attempt to escape led to further violence. On the evening of April 18, they fatally shot Sean Collier, an MIT police officer, in a failed attempt to steal his service weapon. This marked the beginning of a chaotic series of events that included a carjacking and a confrontation with law enforcement in Watertown, Massachusetts. During the Watertown confrontation, the brothers exchanged gunfire with police and Tamerlan was critically injured after being shot multiple times and subsequently run over by his brother as Dzhokhar fled in a stolen vehicle.

The search for Dzhokhar Tsarnaev continued throughout the night and into the following day, leading to an unprecedented lockdown of Boston and surrounding areas. Residents were instructed to stay indoors as law enforcement conducted a door-to-door search. On the evening of April 19, Dzhokhar was found hiding in a boat stored in a backyard. After a brief standoff, he was captured and taken into custody, ending the manhunt.

The investigation into the bombing revealed that the Tsarnaev brothers had acted independently, motivated by extremist Islamic beliefs and anger over U.S. military actions in Muslim countries. The brothers had constructed the bombs using instructions found in an online publication associated with al-Qaeda. However, the investigation also uncovered significant missteps in the handling of intelligence that could have potentially prevented the bombing.

Prior to the attack, the FBI had received warnings from Russian intelligence about Tamerlan Tsarnaev's potential ties to radical Islamist groups. In 2011, the Russian Federal Security Service (FSB) alerted the FBI and the Central Intelligence Agency (CIA) about Tamerlan's activities and requested further investigation. The FBI conducted a limited inquiry, interviewing Tamerlan and his family, but found no evidence of terrorist activity. The case was closed, and Tamerlan was not placed on any watchlist.

However, this information was not adequately shared between agencies or followed up on. The House Homeland Security Committee's investigation into the bombing found that the FBI and the Department of Homeland Security (DHS) had multiple opportunities to investigate Tamerlan more thoroughly and to share critical information with local law enforcement. The lack of communication and coordination between federal and local agencies represented a significant failure in the counterterrorism apparatus.

Additionally, Tamerlan's travel to Russia in 2012, where he spent six months in the volatile region of Dagestan, raised further red flags that were not adequately addressed. Upon his return to the U.S., there were no follow-up investigations despite his known travel to an area with a high level of extremist activity. This gap in monitoring allowed Tamerlan to continue planning the attack without interference.

The bombing and subsequent investigation highlighted several critical areas for improvement in counterterrorism efforts. Firstly, it underscored the need for better intelligence-sharing mechanisms between federal, state, and local law enforcement agencies. Ensuring that relevant information is communicated promptly and acted upon can prevent potential threats from escalating into actual attacks. The Boston Marathon bombing exposed significant weaknesses in this area, leading to reforms aimed at improving coordination and information flow.

Secondly, the importance of community engagement and outreach was brought to the forefront. The Tsarnaev brothers had shown signs of radicalization that were noticed by their community and family members, but these concerns were not effectively communicated to authorities. Building trust and open lines of communication between law enforcement and communities can help identify and mitigate potential threats early.

Thirdly, the incident highlighted the need for continued vigilance in monitoring individuals who have been flagged for potential extremist behavior. While civil liberties must be respected, ensuring that individuals who pose a potential threat are closely monitored and re-evaluated periodically is crucial for public safety. The gaps in monitoring Tamerlan Tsarnaev, especially after his travel to a known hotspot for extremism, represented a significant oversight.

The response to the Boston Marathon bombing also demonstrated the critical importance of emergency preparedness and response capabilities. The swift and effective actions of first responders, medical personnel, and law enforcement were instrumental in saving lives and capturing the perpetrators. The coordination between multiple agencies during the manhunt was a testament to the value of comprehensive training and preparedness for large-scale emergencies.

In the aftermath of the bombing, numerous initiatives were undertaken to enhance security at major public events. Organizers of marathons and other large gatherings implemented stricter security measures, including bag checks, increased law enforcement presence, and surveillance enhancements. These measures aimed to deter potential attacks and ensure a swift response if an incident were to occur.

The Boston Marathon bombing also had a profound impact on the survivors and the broader community. Many of those injured faced long and difficult recoveries, dealing with physical injuries, psychological trauma, and the challenges of adapting to life after the attack. The resilience and solidarity demonstrated by the survivors and the Boston community became a defining narrative in the aftermath of the tragedy. The phrase "Boston Strong" emerged as a symbol of the city's strength, unity, and determination to overcome adversity.

In the legal arena, Dzhokhar Tsarnaev was tried and convicted on multiple charges, including using a weapon of mass destruction and the murder of Officer Sean Collier. In 2015, he was sentenced to death, a decision that was later overturned on appeal but reinstated by the Supreme Court in 2022. The legal proceedings against Tsarnaev sparked debates about the death penalty, the handling of terrorism cases, and the balance between justice and retribution.

The Boston Marathon bombing remains a pivotal event in the history of counterterrorism in the United States. It exposed critical vulnerabilities in the nation's security apparatus and underscored the importance of vigilance, coordination, and preparedness in preventing and responding to terrorist attacks. The lessons learned from this tragedy continue to inform policies and practices aimed at safeguarding public safety and preventing future acts of terror.

Chapter 40: The Amoco Cadiz Oil Spill

The Amoco Cadiz oil spill, which occurred off the coast of Brittany, France, in March 1978, is one of the largest and most environmentally destructive oil spills in history. This maritime disaster had far-reaching ecological, economic, and legal repercussions, highlighting the need for stringent maritime safety protocols and effective oil spill response measures. The incident involved the supertanker Amoco Cadiz, owned by the Amoco Corporation, which ran aground and subsequently broke apart, releasing vast quantities of crude oil into the Atlantic Ocean.

The Amoco Cadiz was a Very Large Crude Carrier (VLCC) measuring over 1,000 feet in length and capable of carrying more than 219,000 tons of crude oil. On March 16, 1978, the vessel was navigating rough seas and high winds en route from the Persian Gulf to Rotterdam, Netherlands, when it encountered mechanical failure. Specifically, the ship's steering mechanism malfunctioned, leaving it adrift and unable to navigate. Despite attempts to regain control and the efforts of tugboats summoned to assist, the Amoco Cadiz ran aground on Portsall Rocks, near the small fishing village of Portsall on the coast of Brittany.

The grounding resulted in the rupture of the tanker's hull, and over the following two weeks, the ship broke apart under the relentless pounding of the waves. Approximately 223,000 tons (about 1.6 million barrels) of light crude oil and 4,000 tons of bunker oil spilled into the sea, forming a massive oil slick that stretched along the coast. The slick ultimately contaminated over 200 miles of the Brittany shoreline, impacting diverse marine and coastal ecosystems.

The environmental impact of the Amoco Cadiz spill was catastrophic. The oil slick affected a wide range of habitats, including rocky shores, sandy beaches, estuaries, and salt marshes. The immediate consequences included the death of thousands of marine animals, such as fish, birds, and invertebrates. The spill devastated local bird populations, with an estimated 300,000 to 400,000 seabirds killed due to oiling. Species such as the common guillemot, razorbill, and puffin suffered severe losses.

The oil also contaminated important breeding and nursery grounds for various marine species. The toxic effects of the oil and the physical smothering of habitats led to long-term ecological damage. Crustaceans, mollusks, and other invertebrates experienced significant mortality rates, disrupting the food web and affecting species that relied on them for sustenance. The contamination of spawning grounds had lasting effects on fish populations, impacting local fisheries for years to come.

The response to the spill was hampered by several factors, including the harsh weather conditions and the sheer scale of the contamination. Initial cleanup efforts focused on preventing the spread of the oil and protecting sensitive areas. Booms and skimmers were deployed, but these measures were largely ineffective against the vast oil slick. Chemical dispersants were used in an attempt to break up the oil, but their effectiveness was limited, and they raised concerns about potential environmental side effects.

The French government, along with international organizations and volunteers, mounted a massive cleanup operation. This involved the removal of oil from beaches and rocks using high-pressure hoses, shovels, and other manual methods. Despite these efforts, the cleanup process was slow and arduous, with oil residues persisting in the environment for many years. The physical removal of oil from the coastline was only part of the challenge; the long-term recovery of affected ecosystems required sustained monitoring and restoration efforts.

The economic impact of the Amoco Cadiz spill on the local community was profound. Brittany's economy relied heavily on fishing, aquaculture, and tourism, all of which were severely disrupted by the spill. The contamination of coastal waters and fishing grounds led to significant financial losses for local fishermen and the collapse of the oyster farming industry in affected areas. The tourism sector also suffered, as oil-covered beaches and polluted waters deterred visitors. The economic repercussions extended beyond immediate losses, with long-term effects on employment and livelihoods in the region.

The Amoco Cadiz disaster had significant legal and regulatory implications. The incident highlighted the need for stricter regulations governing the design, construction, and operation of oil tankers. The lack of redundancy in critical systems, such as the steering mechanism, and the failure to implement adequate safety measures were key factors in the disaster. In response, international maritime regulations were strengthened to enhance the safety and environmental standards for oil tankers.

The legal aftermath of the spill involved extensive litigation. The French government, along with affected local communities and businesses, filed lawsuits against Amoco and related parties, seeking compensation for the environmental damage and economic losses. The legal battle culminated in a landmark decision in 1990, when a U.S. federal court found Amoco and other parties liable for the spill. The court awarded substantial damages, amounting to over $200 million, to cover the costs of cleanup, restoration, and compensation for economic losses. This case set a precedent for holding polluters accountable for environmental disasters and reinforced the principle of the "polluter pays" in international environmental law.

The Amoco Cadiz spill also spurred advancements in oil spill response and preparedness. The disaster underscored the importance of rapid and coordinated response efforts to mitigate the impact of oil spills. In the years following the spill, significant investments were made in developing and improving oil spill response technologies and strategies. This included advancements in oil containment and recovery equipment, the use of more effective dispersants, and the establishment of specialized response teams and protocols.

The incident also led to the establishment of international agreements and organizations focused on preventing and responding to oil spills. One notable outcome was the adoption of the International Convention on Oil Pollution Preparedness, Response and Co-operation (OPRC) in 1990. This convention, developed under the auspices of the International Maritime Organization (IMO), provides a framework for international cooperation in the event of oil pollution incidents and emphasizes the importance of contingency planning and preparedness.

Furthermore, the Amoco Cadiz spill contributed to the development of the European Union's environmental policy framework. The incident highlighted the need for a coordinated European response to environmental disasters and spurred the creation of mechanisms for mutual assistance and cooperation among EU member states. This led to the establishment of the European Maritime Safety Agency (EMSA) in 2002, which plays a key role in supporting oil spill response efforts and enhancing maritime safety across Europe.

The legacy of the Amoco Cadiz oil spill continues to influence environmental policy, maritime safety, and oil spill response practices. The lessons learned from this disaster have informed the development of more robust safety standards and regulatory frameworks aimed at preventing similar incidents. The emphasis on contingency planning, preparedness, and rapid response remains a cornerstone of oil spill management.

In terms of environmental recovery, the affected areas of Brittany have shown remarkable resilience over the decades. While the immediate aftermath of the spill saw extensive ecological damage, natural recovery processes and sustained restoration efforts have contributed to the gradual healing of the coastal and marine ecosystems. The spill underscored the importance of protecting sensitive habitats and the need for ongoing monitoring and conservation efforts to ensure the long-term health of these environments.

The Amoco Cadiz disaster also serves as a poignant reminder of the potential consequences of oil spills for communities and ecosystems. It highlights the complex interplay between human activities, environmental health, and economic well-being. The incident underscores the need for a holistic approach to environmental management that prioritizes prevention, preparedness, and resilience.

Chapter 41: The Thalidomide Tragedy Dosage Mistake

The Thalidomide tragedy, one of the most devastating pharmaceutical disasters in history, stemmed from a catastrophic error in the understanding and administration of a drug that was widely marketed as a safe treatment for a range of ailments, particularly morning sickness in pregnant women. The event stands as a grim reminder of the critical importance of rigorous drug testing, regulatory oversight, and ethical responsibility in the pharmaceutical industry. The thalidomide tragedy resulted in widespread birth defects, leading to an international outcry, significant legal battles, and lasting changes in drug regulation and testing practices.

Thalidomide was first synthesized in 1953 by Chemie Grünenthal, a pharmaceutical company based in West Germany. Initially developed as an anticonvulsant, the drug was found to be ineffective for this purpose but exhibited strong sedative and antiemetic properties. Recognizing its potential, Chemie Grünenthal marketed thalidomide as a treatment for a variety of conditions, including insomnia, anxiety, and nausea. It was particularly promoted as a remedy for morning sickness in pregnant women, and its over-the-counter availability in many countries further facilitated its widespread use.

From 1957 onwards, thalidomide was sold under various brand names, including Contergan in Germany and Distaval in the United Kingdom. The drug was marketed in nearly 50 countries, including major markets in Europe, Australia, Asia, and Canada. The manufacturers touted thalidomide as completely safe, claiming that it was non-toxic and could be used without risk, even in cases of overdose. This was largely based on initial tests conducted on rodents, which suggested that the drug had a high safety margin. However, these tests were grossly inadequate, as they did not include assessments of its effects on fetal development in pregnant women.

The tragedy began to unfold in the late 1950s and early 1960s, when thousands of babies were born with severe deformities, a condition later identified as phocomelia—a rare congenital disorder characterized by limb malformations where the long bones in the arms and legs fail to develop properly. In many cases, the limbs were either extremely shortened or entirely absent, and some infants were born without ears, eyes, or with other severe internal and external deformities. The link between these birth defects and thalidomide was not immediately apparent, as the drug was so widely regarded as safe that doctors and patients did not initially suspect it as the cause of such devastating outcomes.

The scale of the disaster became increasingly clear as reports of birth defects surged across countries where thalidomide was being sold. A critical turning point came in 1961, when Dr. Widukind Lenz, a German pediatrician, and Dr. William McBride, an Australian obstetrician, independently made the connection between the drug and the wave of birth defects. Dr. McBride published a letter in the medical journal The Lancet in December 1961, raising alarm over the correlation between thalidomide use in early pregnancy and severe congenital malformations. This revelation was met with shock and disbelief, but it prompted immediate action from health authorities in several countries, leading to the drug's withdrawal from the market.

By the time thalidomide was withdrawn, an estimated 10,000 to 20,000 babies had been affected worldwide, with roughly 40% of these infants dying shortly after birth due to the severity of their malformations. Survivors faced lifelong physical challenges, including the need for prosthetics, surgeries, and other medical interventions to manage their disabilities. The impact of thalidomide extended beyond the physical; many survivors and their families experienced significant emotional and psychological trauma, exacerbated by the social stigma attached to visible disabilities.

The failure to conduct adequate testing, particularly in pregnant women, was a central cause of the tragedy. Thalidomide was never tested on pregnant animals before it was marketed, a glaring omission that reflected the scientific and ethical standards of the time. This oversight was compounded by the fact that thalidomide crosses the placental barrier, directly affecting the developing fetus. The drug was most teratogenic during the first trimester, a critical period for limb and organ development, when many women might not even be aware they were pregnant. The precise mechanism by which thalidomide caused these defects was not understood at the time, although it is now known to interfere with angiogenesis, the process by which blood vessels form, which is essential for normal limb and organ development.

The regulatory landscape for drug approval in the 1950s and 1960s was far less stringent than it is today. In many countries, drugs could be brought to market with minimal testing, and there was little coordination between different national regulatory bodies. The absence of robust pharmacovigilance systems meant that adverse effects often went unnoticed or unreported until they reached catastrophic levels. In the case of thalidomide, the drug's manufacturers failed to adequately investigate and respond to early reports of side effects, and they continued to market the drug aggressively despite mounting evidence of its dangers.

The legal and financial consequences of the thalidomide disaster were enormous. Survivors and their families pursued compensation through legal channels, leading to protracted legal battles with Chemie Grünenthal and other companies involved in the distribution of the drug. In Germany, the company eventually reached a settlement with victims, providing compensation through a foundation established for this purpose. In the United Kingdom, similar efforts led to the creation of the Thalidomide Trust, which continues to provide financial support and assistance to survivors.

The thalidomide tragedy also had profound implications for the global pharmaceutical industry and drug regulation. In the United States, the Food and Drug Administration (FDA) played a crucial role in preventing the widespread distribution of thalidomide, thanks largely to the efforts of Dr. Frances Kelsey, a pharmacologist and physician who worked at the FDA. Dr. Kelsey was skeptical of the safety data provided by the manufacturers and refused to approve the drug for sale in the U.S., despite significant pressure from the pharmaceutical company. Her actions prevented what could have been an even larger disaster in the United States and earned her widespread acclaim and recognition, including the President's Award for Distinguished Federal Civilian Service from President John F. Kennedy.

The disaster led to significant reforms in drug regulation worldwide. In the United States, the Kefauver-Harris Amendment of 1962 was enacted in response to the thalidomide tragedy. This legislation significantly strengthened the FDA's authority, requiring drug manufacturers to provide substantial evidence of both the safety and efficacy of their products through rigorous clinical trials before they could be approved for sale. The amendment also mandated that drugs be tested for their effects on fetal development, leading to the introduction of more stringent testing protocols and the establishment of guidelines for the safe use of drugs during pregnancy.

Internationally, the thalidomide disaster prompted the creation of more robust regulatory frameworks to prevent similar tragedies. The World Health Organization (WHO) and other international bodies began advocating for stricter standards in drug testing and approval, emphasizing the need for transparency, ethical testing practices, and comprehensive safety assessments. The tragedy also spurred the development of pharmacovigilance systems to monitor and report adverse drug reactions, enabling quicker identification and response to potential safety concerns.

Thalidomide's legacy is complex, as the drug, despite its horrific history, found new applications in the treatment of certain diseases. In the 1990s, researchers discovered that thalidomide had anti-inflammatory and immunomodulatory properties, making it effective in treating conditions such as erythema nodosum leprosum (ENL), a painful complication of leprosy, and multiple myeloma, a type of blood cancer. However, its use is now strictly controlled, with stringent regulations in place to prevent its use during pregnancy and to ensure that patients are fully informed of the risks. The reintroduction of thalidomide in a controlled setting underscores the importance of careful risk-benefit analysis in pharmaceutical development.

The thalidomide tragedy also had a lasting impact on the field of medical ethics, particularly in the areas of informed consent and patient rights. The disaster highlighted the need for transparency and honesty in the doctor-patient relationship, emphasizing that patients must be fully informed of the potential risks and benefits of any treatment. It also underscored the responsibility of pharmaceutical companies to prioritize patient safety over profit and to conduct their research and marketing practices with the highest ethical standards.

For the survivors of thalidomide, the impact of the tragedy is felt every day. Many have had to live with severe physical disabilities, enduring multiple surgeries, chronic pain, and social stigma. The struggle for recognition, compensation, and justice has been a long and difficult journey, with many survivors becoming advocates for disability rights and medical safety. Their resilience and determination have played a crucial role in ensuring that the lessons of thalidomide are not forgotten and that future generations are protected from similar tragedies.

The thalidomide tragedy remains one of the most significant public health disasters of the 20th century, serving as a powerful reminder of the potential consequences of inadequate drug testing and regulation. It has led to lasting changes in the pharmaceutical industry, regulatory practices, and medical ethics, helping to shape the modern landscape of drug development and patient care. The lessons learned from this tragedy continue to inform efforts to ensure that all drugs are safe, effective, and used responsibly, with the health and well-being of patients as the highest priority.

Chapter 42: The Zeebrugge Ferry Capsize

The Zeebrugge ferry capsize, a tragic maritime disaster, occurred on March 6, 1987, when the roll-on/roll-off (Ro-Ro) ferry MS Herald of Free Enterprise capsized shortly after leaving the Belgian port of Zeebrugge. This catastrophe resulted in the loss of 193 lives and brought to light critical deficiencies in maritime safety practices, leading to significant changes in ferry operations and safety regulations.

The MS Herald of Free Enterprise was a modern Ro-Ro ferry operated by Townsend Thoresen, a British ferry company. These types of ferries are designed to allow vehicles to drive on and off the vessel via large bow and stern doors, facilitating rapid loading and unloading. However, this design also posed unique safety challenges, particularly related to the watertight integrity of the vehicle deck. The ferry had a capacity of over 1,300 passengers and around 300 vehicles, making it a crucial link for transport between England and continental Europe.

On the evening of March 6, 1987, the Herald of Free Enterprise departed from Zeebrugge en route to Dover, England, with 539 passengers and crew on board. The ferry set sail at 6:05 PM, despite the fact that the bow doors were not properly closed. This critical oversight was due to a series of failures, both human and systemic. The assistant boatswain, whose responsibility it was to close the bow doors, had fallen asleep in his cabin after working an extended shift. The boatswain himself did not check the status of the doors and proceeded with other duties. The officer on the bridge, who was supposed to ensure that all doors were secure before departure, did not verify the status of the bow doors. Furthermore, there was no alarm system to alert the crew that the doors were open, nor were there any interlocks to prevent the vessel from sailing in such a condition.

As the ferry left the harbor and began to pick up speed, the open bow doors allowed water to flood into the vehicle deck. The free surface effect of the water sloshing around on the vehicle deck caused the vessel to become unstable. Within minutes, the ferry began to list heavily to port. The rapid influx of water led to a catastrophic loss of stability, and the vessel capsized in shallow waters less than a mile from the shore.

The sudden capsize left many passengers and crew trapped inside the ferry as it lay on its side in the cold, dark waters of the English Channel. The chaotic scene was exacerbated by the fact that many passengers were in the ferry's lounges and bars, unaware of the unfolding disaster until it was too late to escape. Those who were able to reach the deck faced the harrowing challenge of navigating the vessel's tilting structure to reach lifeboats and life rafts.

The rescue operation was swift and massive, involving Belgian and British rescue services, military units, and civilian volunteers. Helicopters, lifeboats, and ships converged on the scene to assist survivors and recover bodies. Despite the rapid response, the conditions were challenging, with cold temperatures and rough seas complicating the efforts. Divers were brought in to search the submerged sections of the ferry for survivors, but the cramped, dark, and flooded compartments made their work perilous.

The disaster resulted in the deaths of 193 people, making it one of the worst peacetime maritime tragedies involving a British vessel. The majority of the victims succumbed to drowning or hypothermia, trapped within the ferry's hull. The aftermath of the disaster saw intense public scrutiny and demands for accountability and safety improvements.

A formal investigation into the disaster was launched, led by Mr. Justice Sheen. The resulting report, known as the Sheen Report, provided a detailed analysis of the causes of the capsize and highlighted several critical failures. The report concluded that the primary cause was human error, specifically the failure to close the bow doors. However, it also identified systemic issues within Townsend Thoresen, including poor management practices, inadequate training, and a lack of proper safety protocols. The report was scathing in its criticism, stating that the management of Townsend Thoresen "turned a blind eye" to the need for strict adherence to safety procedures and that the company's culture prioritized speed and efficiency over safety.

The investigation also highlighted the design flaws inherent in Ro-Ro ferries. The open vehicle deck design, while facilitating easy loading and unloading, posed significant risks in the event of flooding. The lack of watertight subdivision within the vehicle deck meant that any water ingress could quickly destabilize the vessel. Furthermore, the absence of safety interlocks to prevent the ship from sailing with open doors, and the lack of alarms to alert the crew to this critical hazard, were significant design and operational oversights.

In the wake of the disaster, Townsend Thoresen rebranded as P&O European Ferries and implemented numerous safety measures across its fleet. These included the installation of indicators and alarms to ensure that all bow and stern doors were securely closed before departure, as well as the introduction of watertight compartments on vehicle decks to limit the spread of water in the event of a breach. Crews were given more rigorous training in emergency procedures, and drills were conducted more frequently to ensure preparedness.

On a broader scale, the International Maritime Organization (IMO) and various national maritime authorities introduced new regulations to improve the safety of Ro-Ro ferries. One of the significant outcomes was the adoption of the SOLAS (Safety of Life at Sea) Convention amendments, which mandated the fitting of indicators, alarms, and monitoring systems for bow, stern, and side doors on Ro-Ro passenger ships. These measures aimed to prevent similar accidents by ensuring that critical safety protocols were followed and by enhancing the overall design safety of these vessels.

The disaster also spurred the development of improved safety standards for passenger evacuation and survivability. This included the design of safer escape routes, better life-saving appliances, and more effective training for both crew and passengers. These changes were aimed at ensuring that in the event of an emergency, passengers and crew would have a better chance of survival.

The legacy of the Zeebrugge disaster extends beyond regulatory changes. The tragedy had a profound impact on the maritime industry, fostering a greater awareness of the importance of safety culture. It underscored the need for rigorous oversight, not only in terms of compliance with regulations but also in fostering an environment where safety is prioritized at all levels of operation. This cultural shift has led to continuous improvements in safety practices and technological advancements that have made modern ferries safer than ever before.

Survivors and the families of the victims played a crucial role in advocating for these changes. Their tireless efforts to seek justice and improve safety standards ensured that the lessons of the Zeebrugge disaster were not forgotten. Many survivors and bereaved families became vocal advocates for maritime safety, contributing to public awareness campaigns and working with regulatory bodies to drive further improvements.

The Zeebrugge ferry capsize remains a poignant reminder of the catastrophic consequences that can result from a combination of human error and systemic failures. The tragedy not only claimed nearly 200 lives but also left a lasting impact on those who survived and the families of the victims. The emotional and psychological scars of the disaster are still felt today, but the resilience and advocacy of the survivors and bereaved families have ensured that the disaster led to meaningful changes that have improved the safety of maritime travel for millions of people worldwide.

Chapter 43: The Collapse of Rana Plaza

The collapse of Rana Plaza on April 24, 2013, in Savar, Bangladesh, stands as one of the deadliest industrial disasters in modern history, shedding light on the extreme risks and exploitative conditions within the global garment industry. The eight-story commercial building housed several garment factories, a bank, apartments, and shops, but it was the garment factories that occupied the majority of the space, employing thousands of workers who produced clothing for numerous Western brands. The disaster not only resulted in a catastrophic loss of life but also prompted a global outcry, leading to significant changes in industry practices and labor rights advocacy.

Rana Plaza was originally designed as a five-story building intended for shops and offices, not industrial use. However, additional floors were illegally added, and heavy machinery for garment production was installed, significantly overloading the building's structural capacity. On April 23, 2013, a day before the collapse, large cracks appeared in the building, prompting an evacuation. Despite this, factory managers, under pressure to meet production deadlines, ordered workers to return to their stations the following day. The decision to reopen the factories proved fatal.

At around 8:57 AM on April 24, 2013, Rana Plaza collapsed, trapping more than 3,500 people inside. The collapse was sudden and catastrophic, reducing the building to a pile of rubble in just 90 seconds. The scene was one of utter devastation, with twisted steel, concrete, and debris making rescue efforts perilous. The screams and cries of those trapped beneath the rubble echoed as rescuers, including local volunteers, emergency services, and military personnel, worked tirelessly to save as many lives as possible. The chaotic environment, compounded by the lack of adequate equipment and training, hampered initial rescue efforts.

In the aftermath, the scale of the disaster became increasingly apparent. The collapse resulted in the deaths of 1,134 people and injured over 2,500, many of whom suffered life-altering injuries such as amputations and severe trauma. The survivors and the families of the victims were left to grapple with profound grief, loss, and the overwhelming burden of medical and financial hardships.

The collapse of Rana Plaza was a stark indictment of the unsafe working conditions prevalent in the garment industry, particularly in countries like Bangladesh, where labor costs are kept low to maintain competitiveness in the global market. Bangladesh is one of the world's largest garment exporters, supplying clothing to numerous international brands and retailers. The industry employs millions of workers, predominantly women, who often face long hours, low wages, and unsafe working conditions. The economic pressures to keep production costs down lead to widespread negligence regarding worker safety and building regulations.

The immediate response to the disaster was characterized by a mix of humanitarian aid and public outrage. International attention quickly turned to the brands and retailers that sourced their products from the factories in Rana Plaza. Consumers, activists, and media outlets demanded accountability and called for significant changes to prevent such tragedies in the future. The scrutiny extended to the entire supply chain, highlighting the often opaque and complex networks that connect Western consumers to workers in developing countries.

The collapse led to the establishment of two major initiatives aimed at improving safety in the Bangladeshi garment industry: the Accord on Fire and Building Safety in Bangladesh and the Alliance for Bangladesh Worker Safety. The Accord, a legally binding agreement between global brands, retailers, and trade unions, aimed to ensure safe working conditions through independent inspections, remediation, and training programs. The Alliance, a similar initiative led by North

American brands, focused on improving safety standards and providing financial support for factory upgrades.

These initiatives brought about tangible improvements, including structural repairs to factories, installation of fire safety equipment, and enhanced worker training on safety protocols. They also increased transparency and accountability within the industry, with public reporting of inspection results and progress updates. However, the implementation of these measures faced numerous challenges, including resistance from factory owners, logistical complexities, and the need for sustained financial investment.

In addition to industry-led efforts, the collapse of Rana Plaza sparked significant activism and advocacy for labor rights. Workers' organizations, NGOs, and international labor unions intensified their efforts to demand fair wages, safe working conditions, and the right to organize. The disaster galvanized a global movement advocating for ethical fashion and responsible sourcing practices, urging consumers to consider the human cost of their clothing choices and to support brands committed to fair labor practices.

The legal aftermath of the collapse saw several high-profile arrests and trials. The owner of Rana Plaza, Sohel Rana, and several factory owners were charged with murder and faced legal proceedings for their role in the disaster. The slow pace of the judicial process and the perceived inadequacies in holding those responsible to account further fueled public discontent and highlighted the systemic issues within the Bangladeshi legal and regulatory framework.

The collapse also had significant economic repercussions for Bangladesh. While the garment industry remains a crucial component of the national economy, the disaster exposed its vulnerabilities and the urgent need for reform. The Bangladeshi government, under pressure from both domestic and international stakeholders, took steps to strengthen labor laws, improve regulatory oversight, and enhance the enforcement of building codes and safety standards. These measures, while necessary, faced ongoing challenges related to corruption, bureaucratic inefficiencies, and the deep-rooted power dynamics within the industry.

For the survivors and the families of the victims, the journey towards recovery has been fraught with difficulties. Compensation schemes were established to provide financial assistance to those affected, funded by contributions from brands, international organizations, and the Bangladeshi government. However, delays and discrepancies in the disbursement of funds led to frustrations and continued hardship for many. The psychological trauma of the disaster, coupled with the physical injuries and economic instability, has left lasting scars on the community.

Despite the progress made in the aftermath of Rana Plaza, the broader challenges facing the global garment industry persist. The drive for fast fashion, characterized by rapid production cycles and low-cost goods, continues to exert pressure on suppliers to cut corners and prioritize profit over worker safety and well-being. The complex and fragmented nature of supply chains complicates efforts to ensure compliance with safety standards and labor rights, necessitating ongoing vigilance and commitment from all stakeholders.

The Rana Plaza disaster serves as a powerful reminder of the human cost of negligence and exploitation within the garment industry. It underscores the need for a collective and sustained effort to prioritize the dignity and safety of workers, to uphold ethical standards, and to foster a culture of accountability and transparency. The tragedy has left an indelible mark on the industry, shaping the discourse around corporate responsibility, consumer awareness, and the pursuit of a more just and equitable global economy.

Chapter 44: The Smolensk Air Disaster Miscommunication

The Smolensk air disaster, which occurred on April 10, 2010, stands as a tragic reminder of the profound consequences of miscommunication and human error in aviation. The crash claimed the lives of all 96 people on board, including Polish President Lech Kaczyński, his wife Maria, and numerous high-ranking Polish officials and military personnel. The delegation was en route to Smolensk, Russia, to attend a commemorative event marking the 70th anniversary of the Katyn massacre, where thousands of Polish officers were executed by the Soviet secret police during World War II. The disaster not only plunged Poland into mourning but also had significant political and diplomatic repercussions, particularly straining Polish-Russian relations.

The aircraft involved was a Tupolev Tu-154M operated by the Polish Air Force. On the morning of the crash, the plane departed from Warsaw Chopin Airport at 7:27 AM local time. The crew was informed of challenging weather conditions at Smolensk North Airport, including dense fog that severely limited visibility. Despite these warnings, the decision was made to proceed to Smolensk, a non-commercial military airport that lacked the sophisticated navigational aids found at larger airports, making it more susceptible to weather-related risks.

As the aircraft approached Smolensk, the crew encountered deteriorating weather conditions with visibility dropping to below the minimums required for a safe landing. The airport's landing aids were limited to non-precision approaches, relying on ground-based navigational aids such as NDBs (Non-Directional Beacons) and VORs (VHF Omnidirectional Range), rather than the more precise ILS (Instrument Landing System) found at major airports. This required greater reliance on visual cues, which were obscured by the fog.

The approach phase is critical in any flight, and it was during this phase that a series of miscommunications and errors occurred. The air traffic controllers at Smolensk North Airport, aware of the poor visibility, repeatedly advised the crew to divert to an alternate airport, such as Vnukovo Airport in Moscow or Minsk Airport in Belarus. However, these suggestions were not heeded. The flight crew, under significant pressure to land at Smolensk due to the importance of the commemorative event and the presence of high-ranking officials, decided to continue with the approach.

One of the primary issues identified in the investigation was the language barrier and procedural discrepancies between the Polish flight crew and the Russian air traffic controllers. The official language of aviation communication is English, but it was reported that conversations occurred in both Russian and Polish, leading to potential misunderstandings. Additionally, the flight crew did not fully adhere to standard operating procedures, and the cockpit environment was marked by a lack of assertiveness and proper decision-making protocols.

The final approach saw the aircraft descending below the glide path, likely due to the crew's attempt to visually acquire the runway in extremely poor visibility. The aircraft's Ground Proximity Warning System (GPWS) issued several warnings, including "Terrain ahead" and "Pull up," but these warnings were not acted upon in a timely manner. The investigation later revealed that the cockpit was a high-stress environment, with the presence of VIP passengers possibly influencing the crew's decisions, as well as the potential for subtle psychological pressure to land despite the risks.

As the aircraft continued its descent, it struck trees approximately 1,100 meters short of the runway, causing significant damage to the left wing. This initial impact led to the aircraft becoming uncontrollable, and it crashed into the ground seconds later, breaking apart and bursting into flames. The crash site was a scene of devastation, with debris scattered over a wide area, complicating rescue and recovery efforts.

The investigation into the Smolensk air disaster was complex and multifaceted, involving both Polish and Russian authorities, as well as international aviation experts. The Russian Interstate Aviation Committee (MAK) conducted the primary investigation, with assistance from Poland's State Commission on Aircraft Accidents Investigation. The final report, released by MAK in January 2011, concluded that the primary cause of the crash was the crew's decision to descend below the minimum descent altitude without having the runway in sight, combined with the adverse weather conditions. Contributing factors included the presence of high-ranking officials in the cockpit, leading to potential psychological pressure on the flight crew, and deficiencies in crew resource management (CRM).

The Polish response to the MAK report was mixed, with some officials accepting the findings, while others, including members of the Polish government and the late president's political party, Law and Justice (PiS), raised concerns about the investigation's impartiality and completeness. They highlighted issues such as potential discrepancies in the radar data, the role of the Russian air traffic controllers, and the adequacy of the Smolensk North Airport's infrastructure.

In response to the disaster, Poland implemented several measures to enhance aviation safety and prevent similar occurrences. These included improving crew training, particularly in the areas of CRM and decision-making under pressure, and reinforcing the importance of adhering to standard operating procedures. Additionally, Poland upgraded its fleet of VIP aircraft and invested in modernizing its aviation infrastructure.

The disaster also had significant diplomatic implications, particularly in the context of Polish-Russian relations. The Katyn massacre, which the delegation was traveling to commemorate, remains a sensitive and contentious historical issue between the two nations.

The Smolensk crash added another layer of complexity to this relationship, with both sides expressing mistrust and dissatisfaction with aspects of the investigation and its conclusions. Efforts to foster reconciliation and cooperation faced setbacks as a result of the disaster and the subsequent handling of the investigation.

Public and political reactions in Poland were intense and polarized. The tragedy deeply affected the Polish people, and the loss of so many prominent figures in a single event created a national trauma. Memorial services and tributes were held across the country, and the victims were honored for their contributions to Poland. The political landscape was also impacted, with the Law and Justice party (PiS) using the disaster as a rallying point to galvanize support and critique the handling of the investigation by the government and international bodies.

Conspiracy theories and alternative explanations for the crash emerged, fueled by political rivalries and public mistrust. Some factions within Poland, particularly supporters of the late President Kaczyński, posited theories of foul play or sabotage, although these claims were not substantiated by the official investigations. The persistence of these theories has contributed to ongoing debates and divisions within Polish society regarding the true nature and causes of the disaster.

The Smolensk air disaster underscored the critical importance of effective communication, rigorous adherence to safety protocols, and the need for robust oversight in aviation operations. It highlighted the vulnerabilities that can arise when human factors, such as psychological pressure and decision-making under stress, intersect with technical and procedural shortcomings. The lessons learned from this tragedy have informed global aviation practices, emphasizing the need for continuous improvement in training, communication, and safety management.

Chapter 45: The SpaceX CRS-7 Mission Failure

The SpaceX CRS-7 mission failure on June 28, 2015, was a significant event in the history of space exploration, highlighting the challenges and risks associated with spaceflight and the complexities of modern rocket technology. The failure of this mission, which was part of NASA's Commercial Resupply Services (CRS) program, had widespread implications for the space industry, affected the International Space Station (ISS) supply chain, and led to detailed investigations and changes in engineering practices and safety protocols.

SpaceX, founded by Elon Musk in 2002, had quickly risen to prominence as a key player in the space industry, pioneering reusable rocket technology and securing contracts with NASA and other entities for launching payloads into space. The CRS-7 mission, using the Falcon 9 rocket, was intended to deliver critical supplies and equipment to the ISS. This included food, scientific experiments, and an important piece of hardware called the International Docking Adapter (IDA), which was crucial for future docking operations with crewed spacecraft.

The Falcon 9 rocket, known for its innovative design and capability to return its first stage booster to Earth for reuse, had a series of successful launches prior to CRS-7, building confidence in SpaceX's technology and operations. The launch of CRS-7 took place at Cape Canaveral Air Force Station in Florida, with a scheduled liftoff time of 10:21 AM EDT. The initial phases of the launch proceeded as planned, with the rocket clearing the launch pad and ascending through the atmosphere.

Approximately two minutes and 19 seconds into the flight, as the rocket was experiencing maximum aerodynamic pressure, an anomaly occurred. The upper stage of the Falcon 9 began to disintegrate, leading to the catastrophic loss of the vehicle and its payload. The failure was sudden and dramatic, with the rocket breaking apart and debris falling into the Atlantic Ocean. Telemetry data was lost shortly after the anomaly, and it was clear that the mission had ended in failure.

The immediate aftermath of the failure was marked by shock and disappointment among SpaceX and NASA teams, as well as the broader space community. The loss of the CRS-7 mission represented a significant setback for SpaceX, which had been on a streak of successful launches, and for NASA, which relied on commercial partners to maintain the supply chain to the ISS. The failure also raised concerns about the reliability and safety of commercial spaceflight, prompting a thorough investigation to determine the cause and prevent future occurrences.

SpaceX, in collaboration with NASA and the Federal Aviation Administration (FAA), launched an extensive investigation into the failure. The investigation involved detailed analysis of telemetry data, debris recovery and examination, and rigorous testing of hardware components. The primary focus was to identify the root cause of the anomaly and understand the sequence of events that led to the destruction of the rocket.

After several months of investigation, SpaceX announced the findings in a detailed report. The root cause of the CRS-7 failure was traced to a structural failure in one of the composite overwrapped pressure vessels (COPVs) inside the rocket's second stage liquid oxygen (LOX) tank. COPVs are used to store helium at high pressure, which is then used to pressurize the propellant tanks during flight. The investigation revealed that a strut holding one of the COPVs in place had fractured, causing the vessel to break free and leading to the rapid release of helium into the LOX tank.

This sudden release of helium created an overpressure event that caused the second stage LOX tank to rupture, leading to the disintegration of the upper stage and the subsequent loss of the vehicle. The investigation identified that the strut, provided by an external supplier, had failed at a lower load than its certified rating. This failure was attributed to a manufacturing defect, which had gone undetected during quality control inspections.

The findings of the investigation prompted several changes in SpaceX's engineering practices and quality assurance processes. One of the key changes was the decision to bring the manufacturing of critical components like the struts in-house, allowing for greater control over the quality and reliability of these parts. SpaceX also implemented more rigorous testing and inspection protocols to ensure that all components met the necessary standards for spaceflight.

In addition to these internal changes, SpaceX worked closely with NASA and other stakeholders to enhance the overall safety and reliability of their launch operations. This included improvements to the design and testing of COPVs, as well as updates to the Falcon 9 rocket to incorporate lessons learned from the CRS-7 failure. These efforts were aimed at preventing similar incidents in the future and restoring confidence in SpaceX's ability to conduct safe and reliable space missions.

The impact of the CRS-7 failure extended beyond SpaceX and NASA, affecting the broader space industry and the ISS program. The loss of the mission delayed the delivery of critical supplies and equipment to the ISS, necessitating adjustments to the station's operations and resupply schedule. NASA and its international partners had to rely on other cargo missions, including those by Orbital ATK and the Russian Progress spacecraft, to maintain the flow of supplies to the ISS.

The failure also had financial implications for SpaceX, which faced the costs of the lost mission and the expenses associated with the investigation and corrective actions. Despite these challenges, SpaceX's resilience and commitment to addressing the issues demonstrated the company's dedication to advancing space technology and ensuring the safety and success of future missions.

The CRS-7 failure also had broader implications for the commercialization of space. The incident underscored the inherent risks of spaceflight and the importance of robust engineering and quality control practices. It also highlighted the need for effective collaboration between commercial entities and government agencies to ensure the safety and reliability of space missions. The lessons learned from CRS-7 contributed to the ongoing efforts to develop a sustainable and reliable commercial space industry.

In the aftermath of the CRS-7 failure, SpaceX focused on returning to flight with enhanced safety measures and improved designs. The company conducted a series of successful launches in the following months, culminating in the successful launch of the CRS-8 mission on April 8, 2016. This mission marked the return to flight for SpaceX's Falcon 9 rocket and successfully delivered supplies and scientific experiments to the ISS. The CRS-8 mission also demonstrated the successful recovery of the first stage booster, a key milestone in SpaceX's efforts to develop reusable rocket technology.

The successful return to flight and subsequent missions reinforced SpaceX's position as a leader in the commercial space industry and restored confidence in the company's capabilities. The experience of the CRS-7 failure and the subsequent improvements also contributed to the ongoing development of SpaceX's Crew Dragon spacecraft, which would later be used for crewed missions to the ISS under NASA's Commercial Crew Program.

The CRS-7 failure serves as a reminder of the challenges and risks inherent in space exploration and the importance of continuous improvement in engineering, quality control, and risk management. The incident and its aftermath highlight the resilience and dedication of the teams involved, as well as the critical role of collaboration and transparency in addressing failures and advancing the field of space exploration.

Chapter 46: The 2001 Enron Accounting Scandal

The 2001 Enron accounting scandal is one of the most infamous and far-reaching corporate frauds in American history. It led to the bankruptcy of Enron Corporation, a Houston-based energy company, and the dissolution of Arthur Andersen, one of the five largest audit and accountancy partnerships in the world. The scandal brought to light the extent of corporate greed and the failure of regulatory bodies, shaking public confidence in corporate governance and financial reporting. The aftermath of the scandal led to significant changes in regulations and practices governing corporate accounting and auditing in the United States.

Enron was established in 1985 through the merger of Houston Natural Gas and InterNorth. Under the leadership of Kenneth Lay, who served as CEO, Enron transformed from a traditional energy company into a diversified corporation engaged in various trading markets. Enron's business model involved buying and selling natural gas and electricity futures and derivatives, which were financial instruments used to hedge against price fluctuations. By the 1990s, Enron had expanded into various other markets, including broadband, weather derivatives, and even water trading.

The company was hailed as an innovator, and its stock price soared throughout the 1990s. Enron's revenue grew from $9 billion in 1995 to over $100 billion in 2000, making it the seventh-largest company in the United States. However, much of this growth was built on a foundation of financial manipulation and fraudulent accounting practices.

At the heart of the Enron scandal was the use of special purpose entities (SPEs), also known as special purpose vehicles (SPVs). These off-balance-sheet partnerships were used to hide Enron's debt and inflate its earnings. The company created hundreds of these SPEs, which were ostensibly independent but were, in reality, controlled by Enron. The SPEs were used to transfer debt and underperforming assets off Enron's balance sheet, making the company's financial position appear stronger than it actually was.

One of the most infamous SPEs was the LJM partnership, managed by Enron's Chief Financial Officer (CFO) Andrew Fastow. LJM and other similar entities allowed Enron to move poorly performing assets off its books and recognize revenue from sales to these entities, even though the transactions were essentially shams. This created the illusion of high profitability and rapid growth, which in turn inflated Enron's stock price.

The accounting firm Arthur Andersen played a crucial role in the scandal. As Enron's auditor, Andersen was responsible for reviewing and certifying the company's financial statements. However, Andersen failed to perform its duties with due diligence and independence. The firm not only failed to catch the irregularities in Enron's accounting practices but also actively assisted in structuring some of the SPE transactions. This cozy relationship was partly due to the fact that Andersen was earning substantial fees from both auditing and consulting services provided to Enron.

The unraveling of Enron began in 2001 when the company's complex web of financial manipulation started to come to light. In August 2001, CEO Jeffrey Skilling resigned unexpectedly, citing personal reasons. Skilling's departure raised suspicions, and soon after, a series of revelations began to emerge. Enron's stock price, which had peaked at around $90 per share in mid-2000, began to decline rapidly.

In October 2001, Enron announced that it was taking a $1 billion charge against earnings, primarily due to losses from its SPEs. This disclosure led to increased scrutiny from analysts, investors, and regulators. The U.S. Securities and Exchange Commission (SEC) launched an investigation into Enron's accounting practices. The company also admitted that it had overstated its earnings by nearly $600 million over the previous four years.

As the investigations progressed, it became clear that Enron's financial position was far worse than initially disclosed. In November 2001, the company announced that it had overstated its earnings by an additional $586 million since 1997. This admission further eroded investor confidence, and Enron's stock price continued to plummet. By December 2001, Enron filed for bankruptcy, marking the largest corporate bankruptcy in U.S. history at that time.

The fallout from the Enron scandal was extensive. Thousands of employees lost their jobs and retirement savings, as much of their 401(k) investments were tied up in Enron stock. Investors lost billions of dollars as the company's stock became worthless. The scandal also had a profound impact on the accounting profession, leading to the dissolution of Arthur Andersen. In June 2002, Andersen was convicted of obstruction of justice for shredding documents related to its audit of Enron, effectively putting the firm out of business.

In response to the Enron scandal and other corporate frauds that emerged around the same time, the U.S. Congress enacted the Sarbanes-Oxley Act (SOX) in July 2002. SOX aimed to restore public confidence in corporate governance and financial reporting by implementing stricter regulations and oversight. Key provisions of SOX included the establishment of the Public Company Accounting Oversight Board (PCAOB) to oversee the auditing profession, the requirement for CEOs and CFOs to certify the accuracy of financial statements, and enhanced disclosure requirements for off-balance-sheet transactions and insider trading.

The Sarbanes-Oxley Act also introduced stricter penalties for corporate fraud and expanded protections for whistleblowers. It required companies to establish internal controls and procedures for financial reporting and mandated that external auditors assess the effectiveness of these controls. The act significantly increased the accountability of corporate executives, boards of directors, and auditors, aiming to prevent future accounting scandals and restore integrity to the financial markets.

The Enron scandal also had broader implications for corporate governance practices. It highlighted the need for greater transparency, ethical conduct, and independent oversight in corporate operations. Many companies re-evaluated their governance structures, strengthening the roles of independent directors and audit committees. The scandal underscored the importance of fostering a corporate culture that prioritizes ethical behavior and long-term value creation over short-term financial gains.

Several key figures in the Enron scandal faced legal consequences. Jeffrey Skilling, Enron's former CEO, was convicted in 2006 on multiple counts of conspiracy, fraud, and insider trading. He was sentenced to 24 years in prison, though his sentence was later reduced to 14 years as part of a settlement agreement. Andrew Fastow, Enron's CFO, pleaded guilty to charges of conspiracy and fraud, cooperating with prosecutors in exchange for a reduced sentence. He was sentenced to six years in prison.

Kenneth Lay, Enron's founder and former chairman, was also indicted on multiple charges of fraud and conspiracy. However, Lay died of a heart attack in July 2006, before he could be sentenced. Lay's death meant that his conviction was vacated, as he did not have the opportunity to exhaust his appeals.

The Enron scandal remains a cautionary tale about the dangers of corporate greed, unethical behavior, and the failure of oversight mechanisms. It demonstrated how complex financial instruments and off-balance-sheet entities could be used to obscure a company's true financial health, misleading investors and regulators. The scandal also highlighted the potential for conflicts of interest in the relationship between auditors and their clients, underscoring the need for independence and objectivity in the auditing process.

In the years following the Enron scandal, the financial markets experienced other significant crises, such as the global financial crisis of 2007-2008. These events further reinforced the importance of strong regulatory frameworks, effective corporate governance, and ethical behavior in maintaining the stability and integrity of the financial system.

Chapter 47: The L'Aquila Earthquake Prediction Error

The L'Aquila earthquake prediction error in 2009 serves as a significant case study in the complexities and challenges of earthquake prediction, the responsibilities of scientists and government officials in communicating risks, and the legal and ethical ramifications of those communications. This event, which involved the miscommunication and misinterpretation of seismic risk assessments, had profound consequences for the affected community, the scientific community, and legal frameworks regarding natural disaster prediction and response.

L'Aquila, a historic city in central Italy, sits in a region known for its seismic activity. On April 6, 2009, at 3:32 AM local time, a magnitude 6.3 earthquake struck the area, causing widespread devastation. The quake resulted in the deaths of 309 people, injured more than 1,500, and left tens of thousands homeless. The destruction included the collapse of many buildings, including historical structures, homes, and schools, and caused extensive economic and emotional damage to the community.

In the weeks leading up to the earthquake, the region experienced numerous small tremors, known as seismic swarms. These minor quakes raised concerns among the local population about the possibility of a larger, more destructive earthquake. In response to these concerns, the Italian Department of Civil Protection convened a meeting of the National Commission for the Forecast and Prevention of Major Risks on March 31, 2009, just six days before the earthquake. This commission comprised leading seismologists, geophysicists, and other experts in earthquake science.

The purpose of the meeting was to assess the seismic activity and provide guidance on the potential risk of a major earthquake. The scientists at the meeting concluded that while the seismic swarm was indicative of increased seismic activity, it did not necessarily mean that a major earthquake was imminent. They emphasized the uncertainty inherent in earthquake prediction, noting that it is impossible to predict precisely when and where an earthquake will occur. This nuanced understanding of seismic risk, however, was not effectively communicated to the public.

Following the meeting, government officials, including Bernardo De Bernardinis, then deputy head of the Civil Protection Department, conveyed reassurances to the public. In a widely publicized statement, De Bernardinis suggested that the ongoing tremors were relieving seismic pressure and reducing the likelihood of a major earthquake. This statement was interpreted by many residents as an assurance that a major earthquake was not imminent, leading some to remain in their homes rather than evacuate.

When the earthquake struck on April 6, the resulting devastation and loss of life led to outrage and accusations of negligence and miscommunication against the scientists and officials involved. Survivors and victims' families argued that the reassurances provided by the commission and the Civil Protection Department had misled them, contributing to the high death toll and extensive damage. The perceived failure to adequately warn the public and take precautionary measures became the focal point of a highly controversial legal case.

In 2010, seven members of the National Commission for the Forecast and Prevention of Major Risks, along with De Bernardinis, were charged with manslaughter and negligence. The prosecution argued that the experts had provided incomplete, inaccurate, and falsely reassuring information to the public, which had influenced people's decisions and resulted in preventable deaths. The trial, which began in September 2011, garnered international attention and sparked intense debate within the scientific and legal communities.

The trial centered on the complex interplay between scientific uncertainty, risk communication, and public perception. The defense argued that earthquake prediction is inherently uncertain and that the scientists had acted responsibly by providing a nuanced assessment of the risks. They emphasized that the commission had not predicted the earthquake but had merely assessed the likelihood based on available data, which did not indicate an imminent major quake. The defense also highlighted that effective risk communication is challenging, especially when dealing with probabilistic information and public expectations.

Despite these arguments, in October 2012, the court found the defendants guilty of manslaughter and sentenced them to six years in prison. The verdict was widely criticized by the scientific community, which viewed it as a dangerous precedent that could discourage scientists from engaging in risk assessment and communication for fear of legal repercussions. The case raised concerns about the criminalization of scientific advice and the implications for public trust in scientific institutions.

The verdict was appealed, and in November 2014, an appellate court overturned the convictions of six of the scientists, while upholding the conviction of De Bernardinis. The court ruled that the scientists had not provided reassurances but had instead conveyed the inherent uncertainties in earthquake prediction. De Bernardinis' conviction was upheld on the grounds that his public statements had been overly reassuring and had not adequately reflected the commission's nuanced assessment. This outcome underscored the importance of careful and accurate communication of scientific risk assessments to the public.

The L'Aquila earthquake prediction error and subsequent legal proceedings had significant implications for the scientific community and public policy. One of the key lessons was the need for effective communication strategies that convey the uncertainties and complexities of scientific risk assessments to the public. This includes ensuring that government officials and spokespersons accurately represent the findings and recommendations of scientific experts, without oversimplifying or misinterpreting the information.

The case also highlighted the ethical responsibilities of scientists and officials in communicating risks. While it is essential to provide the public with accurate and timely information, it is equally important to avoid creating false assurances or undue panic. Balancing these considerations requires a nuanced understanding of both the scientific data and the social context in which the information is communicated.

In response to the L'Aquila case, efforts were made to improve risk communication and public understanding of seismic hazards. The Italian government and scientific institutions implemented measures to enhance the transparency and accuracy of risk assessments. This included developing clearer guidelines for communicating probabilistic information and engaging with the public in a more interactive and informative manner. Additionally, there was an emphasis on educating the public about the inherent uncertainties in earthquake prediction and the importance of preparedness and resilience.

The L'Aquila earthquake also prompted broader discussions about the role of scientists in public policy and the potential legal and ethical implications of their work. The case underscored the need for a supportive legal framework that protects scientists from undue liability while ensuring accountability and transparency in risk assessment and communication. It also highlighted the importance of fostering a culture of trust and collaboration between scientists, government officials, and the public.

In the years following the L'Aquila earthquake, advancements in seismic monitoring and risk assessment have continued to improve our understanding of earthquake hazards. Technologies such as early warning systems, enhanced seismic networks, and improved modeling techniques have contributed to more accurate and timely assessments of seismic risks. These advancements, combined with improved communication strategies, aim to enhance public safety and resilience in the face of natural disasters.

Chapter 48: The Teton Dam Collapse

The Teton Dam collapse on June 5, 1976, stands as one of the most catastrophic dam failures in U.S. history, marking a profound tragedy in terms of human loss, property damage, and environmental impact. Located in southeastern Idaho, the dam was intended to serve multiple purposes, including irrigation, flood control, and hydroelectric power generation. However, its sudden and dramatic failure highlighted significant flaws in its design, construction, and the oversight practices of the time. This event underscores the critical importance of rigorous engineering, thorough geological analysis, and stringent construction standards in large-scale infrastructure projects.

The Teton Dam was a part of the Bureau of Reclamation's ambitious projects aimed at supporting agricultural development in the arid regions of the American West. The idea of constructing the dam was first proposed in the 1930s, but it wasn't until the 1960s that the project gained momentum. The dam was designed as an earthen embankment structure, standing 305 feet high and 0.6 miles long, and intended to impound the Teton River, creating a reservoir with a storage capacity of approximately 288,000 acre-feet.

Construction of the Teton Dam began in 1972 and was completed in November 1975. The dam was built using a zoned earthfill design, which involved using different types of soil and rock materials placed in distinct zones to achieve the necessary structural integrity and stability. The core of the dam was made of impervious materials to prevent water seepage, while the outer shells were composed of more permeable materials for support and stability. The dam also featured a spillway and outlet works designed to manage water flow and prevent overtopping.

From the outset, the Teton Dam project faced numerous challenges, particularly concerning the geological conditions of the site. The area around the Teton River is characterized by complex geology, including layers of volcanic ash, rhyolite, and basalt, interspersed with fractures and fissures. These conditions posed significant risks for seepage and stability, which required careful consideration in the design and construction phases. However, some of these geological risks were not adequately addressed, leading to vulnerabilities in the dam's integrity.

The first signs of trouble appeared as the reservoir began to fill in the spring of 1976. Small leaks were observed in the downstream face of the dam, but these were initially considered manageable and not indicative of a severe problem. However, the situation rapidly deteriorated on June 5, 1976, when a small leak on the downstream side of the dam suddenly escalated. At around 7:30 AM, water began to seep through the dam, quickly developing into a significant flow. Despite frantic efforts by construction crews to plug the leak, the erosion intensified, and by 11:57 AM, a large section of the dam collapsed, unleashing a catastrophic flood downstream.

The breach of the Teton Dam released an estimated 80 billion gallons of water into the Teton River Valley, creating a massive flood wave that devastated everything in its path. The torrent of water surged downstream, sweeping away homes, farms, livestock, and infrastructure. The towns of Wilford, Sugar City, Rexburg, and Idaho Falls were among the hardest hit, with Rexburg suffering extensive damage. In total, the floodwaters inundated over 300 square miles of land, causing widespread destruction and displacing thousands of people.

The human cost of the disaster was significant. Although the loss of life was relatively low compared to the scale of the flood, with 11 people and 13,000 cattle killed, the impact on the affected communities was profound. Many residents lost their homes, possessions, and livelihoods. The psychological and emotional toll on the survivors was immense, as they faced the daunting task of rebuilding their lives in the aftermath of the flood.

The economic impact of the Teton Dam collapse was staggering. The immediate damage was estimated at around $400 million in 1976 dollars (equivalent to over $1.7 billion today), with long-term economic losses far exceeding this amount. The disaster disrupted agricultural production, destroyed infrastructure, and necessitated extensive relief and recovery efforts. The federal government, through the Bureau of Reclamation and other agencies, provided substantial aid to the affected communities, but the process of recovery was slow and arduous.

In the aftermath of the collapse, a comprehensive investigation was launched to determine the causes of the failure and to prevent similar disasters in the future. The investigation, led by the Independent Panel to Review Cause of Teton Dam Failure, uncovered a series of critical issues that contributed to the catastrophe. One of the primary factors was inadequate consideration of the geological conditions at the dam site. The porous and fractured rock formations underlying the dam allowed water to seep through, undermining the structure's integrity.

The investigation also revealed significant flaws in the design and construction of the dam. The core material used in the dam was found to be highly susceptible to erosion when exposed to water, and the design did not include adequate measures to prevent seepage through the foundation and abutments. Additionally, the construction quality control was insufficient, with reports of rushed work, inadequate compaction of materials, and insufficient attention to potential seepage paths.

Another critical factor was the lack of effective oversight and communication among the various entities involved in the project. The Bureau of Reclamation, which oversaw the construction, failed to adequately address the concerns raised by its own engineers and geologists regarding the site's suitability and the potential risks. The project's urgency and the pressure to complete it on time and within budget further exacerbated these issues, leading to compromised safety standards.

The findings of the investigation led to significant changes in dam safety practices and policies. One of the most important outcomes was the establishment of more rigorous standards for dam design, construction, and maintenance. The Bureau of Reclamation and other agencies involved in dam construction adopted stricter guidelines for site selection, geological assessment, and material testing. These measures were aimed at ensuring that the lessons learned from the Teton Dam disaster would be applied to prevent future failures.

The Teton Dam collapse also underscored the importance of emergency preparedness and response. The disaster highlighted the need for effective communication and coordination among federal, state, and local agencies to manage such emergencies. The establishment of comprehensive emergency action plans for dams and other critical infrastructure became a priority, with an emphasis on early warning systems, evacuation procedures, and public awareness campaigns.

In the years following the Teton Dam collapse, dam safety programs were significantly enhanced across the United States. The National Dam Safety Program, established by the Federal Emergency Management Agency (FEMA) in 1979, provided a framework for improving dam safety nationwide. The program emphasized regular inspections, maintenance, and upgrades for existing dams, as well as stringent standards for new dam construction. These efforts aimed to ensure that the nation's dams would be safer and more reliable, protecting both human lives and valuable resources.

The legacy of the Teton Dam disaster continues to influence engineering practices and policies today. The lessons learned from the collapse have been incorporated into engineering education, professional standards, and regulatory frameworks. The emphasis on thorough geological analysis, rigorous design and construction standards, and effective oversight has become ingrained in the field of civil engineering, helping to prevent similar tragedies in the future.

Chapter 49: The 2010 San Bruno Pipeline Explosion

The 2010 San Bruno pipeline explosion is a stark reminder of the potential dangers associated with aging infrastructure and the critical importance of rigorous maintenance, inspection, and regulation of utility systems. On September 9, 2010, a natural gas pipeline operated by Pacific Gas and Electric Company (PG&E) ruptured in the suburban neighborhood of San Bruno, California, resulting in a massive explosion and fire that caused extensive damage, loss of life, and long-lasting impacts on the community. This disaster brought to light serious deficiencies in pipeline management practices and led to significant regulatory changes aimed at improving the safety and reliability of natural gas infrastructure.

San Bruno, located just south of San Francisco, is a densely populated area with residential homes, schools, and businesses. The natural gas pipeline that exploded, known as Line 132, was part of PG&E's extensive network serving the region. This particular pipeline was installed in 1956 and was a high-pressure transmission line, designed to transport natural gas from storage facilities to distribution networks that served homes and businesses. As with many pieces of critical infrastructure, the pipeline had aged over the decades, raising concerns about its integrity and safety.

On the evening of September 9, 2010, at approximately 6:11 PM, Line 132 ruptured, releasing a massive volume of natural gas into the surrounding area. The escaping gas quickly ignited, resulting in an explosion that was so powerful it registered as a 1.1 magnitude seismic event on local monitoring equipment. The blast created a fireball that reached hundreds of feet into the air, engulfing the surrounding neighborhood in flames. The explosion and ensuing fire destroyed 38 homes and damaged many others, creating a scene of chaos and devastation.

The immediate human toll of the disaster was severe. Eight people lost their lives, and dozens more were injured, some critically. The explosion and fire forced the evacuation of hundreds of residents, many of whom lost their homes and all their possessions. The psychological and emotional impact on the survivors and the community as a whole was profound, as they struggled to come to terms with the sudden and violent destruction of their neighborhood.

First responders, including firefighters, police officers, and emergency medical personnel, faced enormous challenges in managing the disaster. The intensity of the fire, fueled by the continuous release of natural gas from the ruptured pipeline, made it difficult to control the blaze. It took hours to shut off the gas supply and bring the fire under control. The efforts of the first responders were heroic, as they worked tirelessly to rescue residents, extinguish the flames, and prevent further loss of life and property.

In the aftermath of the explosion, attention quickly turned to understanding the cause of the rupture and preventing similar incidents in the future. The National Transportation Safety Board (NTSB) launched an extensive investigation to determine the root causes of the disaster. The investigation revealed a series of critical failures and deficiencies in PG&E's management of its natural gas pipeline system.

One of the primary issues identified was the inadequate maintenance and inspection of Line 132. The pipeline had numerous defects and weaknesses that had gone undetected or unaddressed over the years. The NTSB found that the section of the pipeline that ruptured had a defective weld that was not properly documented or repaired. This weld failure was a significant factor in the pipeline's rupture, and it highlighted broader problems with PG&E's record-keeping and maintenance practices.

The investigation also uncovered deficiencies in PG&E's pipeline safety management program. The company had not conducted sufficient risk assessments to identify and mitigate potential hazards associated with its aging infrastructure. Additionally, PG&E's emergency response procedures were found to be inadequate, as there were delays and confusion in shutting off the gas supply and coordinating the response to the explosion. These shortcomings exacerbated the severity of the disaster and underscored the need for more robust safety protocols and emergency planning.

Another critical issue identified by the NTSB was the lack of effective regulatory oversight. The California Public Utilities Commission (CPUC), which is responsible for regulating utility companies in the state, had not enforced stringent safety standards or conducted thorough inspections of PG&E's pipeline system. This regulatory gap allowed PG&E's deficiencies to go unchecked, contributing to the conditions that led to the explosion.

The findings of the NTSB investigation led to significant legal, regulatory, and financial repercussions for PG&E. The company faced numerous lawsuits from victims and their families, resulting in substantial settlements and compensation payments. Additionally, PG&E was subjected to fines and penalties from regulatory agencies, and its reputation was severely damaged. The disaster also prompted a broader public and political outcry, leading to calls for sweeping reforms in pipeline safety and utility regulation.

In response to the San Bruno explosion, federal and state authorities implemented a series of regulatory changes aimed at enhancing the safety and reliability of natural gas pipelines. The Pipeline and Hazardous Materials Safety Administration (PHMSA), the federal agency responsible for pipeline safety, introduced new regulations requiring more rigorous inspection and maintenance standards for pipeline operators. These regulations mandated regular integrity assessments, enhanced record-keeping, and more comprehensive risk management practices.

At the state level, the CPUC undertook significant reforms to improve its oversight of utility companies. The commission strengthened its safety regulations, increased its inspection and enforcement activities, and enhanced its emergency response capabilities. Additionally, the CPUC established new requirements for utility companies to develop and implement comprehensive pipeline safety plans, including measures to address aging infrastructure and mitigate potential risks.

The San Bruno disaster also led to technological advancements in pipeline monitoring and safety. Utility companies began adopting more advanced technologies, such as automated shut-off valves, real-time monitoring systems, and enhanced leak detection methods. These technologies aimed to improve the ability to detect and respond to pipeline failures more quickly, reducing the risk of catastrophic incidents.

PG&E, in particular, faced significant scrutiny and pressure to reform its practices in the wake of the explosion. The company launched a comprehensive pipeline safety enhancement program, investing billions of dollars in upgrading its infrastructure, improving its maintenance procedures, and enhancing its emergency response capabilities. PG&E also worked to rebuild trust with the affected communities, engaging in outreach and communication efforts to address the concerns of residents and stakeholders.

The legacy of the 2010 San Bruno pipeline explosion extends beyond the immediate aftermath of the disaster. The incident served as a catalyst for broader changes in the utility industry, highlighting the importance of proactive safety management, rigorous regulatory oversight, and continuous improvement in infrastructure practices. The lessons learned from San Bruno continue to inform efforts to enhance the safety and reliability of natural gas pipelines across the United States.

Chapter 50: The St. Francis Dam Failure

The St. Francis Dam failure on March 12, 1928, remains one of the most catastrophic civil engineering disasters in United States history. The collapse of the dam, located in the San Francisquito Canyon in Los Angeles County, California, resulted in the deaths of at least 431 people and caused extensive property damage. This tragic event highlighted significant deficiencies in dam design, construction practices, and oversight, leading to profound changes in engineering standards and public policy regarding the safety and management of large infrastructure projects.

The St. Francis Dam was conceived as part of an ambitious plan to provide a reliable water supply to the growing city of Los Angeles. During the early 20th century, Los Angeles was rapidly expanding, and the demand for water was outstripping the available supply. The Los Angeles Aqueduct, completed in 1913 under the leadership of William Mulholland, had already brought water from the Owens Valley to the city, but additional storage capacity was needed to ensure a consistent supply during periods of low rainfall. The St. Francis Dam was intended to serve as a critical reservoir, storing water diverted from the Owens River for use during dry periods.

Construction of the St. Francis Dam began in 1924 and was completed in 1926. The dam was an arch-gravity type, designed to hold back a reservoir with a capacity of approximately 38,000 acre-feet. Standing 205 feet high and 600 feet long, the dam was constructed primarily of concrete. The design was overseen by William Mulholland, the chief engineer and general manager of the Los Angeles Department of Water and Power (LADWP), who was widely regarded as a pioneer in the field of water management.

From the outset, the St. Francis Dam project faced several challenges and controversies. One of the primary issues was the suitability of the site chosen for the dam. The San Francisquito Canyon was characterized by complex geology, including layers of sedimentary rock, schist, and alluvial deposits, which posed significant risks for the stability of the structure. Despite these concerns, the project proceeded without a comprehensive geological survey or thorough evaluation of the potential hazards.

As the dam was constructed, several warning signs emerged that suggested potential problems with the structure. Cracks and leaks were observed in the dam's foundation and abutments, indicating that the underlying rock and soil were not as stable as initially believed. Additionally, there were reports of seepage through the dam, which was initially dismissed as normal behavior for a concrete structure. Mulholland and his team took steps to address these issues, including grouting and other repairs, but the fundamental vulnerabilities of the site were not fully understood or mitigated.

On the evening of March 12, 1928, just before midnight, the St. Francis Dam suddenly and catastrophically failed. The exact cause of the collapse remains a subject of debate, but it is generally believed that a combination of factors, including the instability of the underlying rock formations, inadequate design, and construction deficiencies, contributed to the failure. The collapse released a wall of water, estimated at 12.4 billion gallons, which surged down the San Francisquito Canyon and into the Santa Clara River Valley.

The floodwaters traveled at an estimated speed of 18 miles per hour, devastating everything in their path. The torrent of water destroyed homes, farms, bridges, and infrastructure, creating a trail of destruction that extended more than 50 miles to the Pacific Ocean. The towns of Castaic Junction, Piru, Fillmore, Bardsdale, and Santa Paula were among the hardest hit, with many residents caught off guard by the sudden and overwhelming flood. The force of the water was so powerful that it carried debris, including large boulders and entire buildings, for miles downstream.

The human toll of the disaster was immense. At least 431 people lost their lives, making it one of the deadliest dam failures in U.S. history. Many of the victims were migrant workers and their families living in makeshift camps along the river, who had little warning of the impending flood. The bodies of the victims were found as far away as the Pacific Ocean, illustrating the magnitude of the flood's impact. The disaster also caused significant property damage, with estimates of the economic loss reaching $7 million (equivalent to over $100 million today).

In the immediate aftermath of the collapse, rescue and recovery efforts were launched by local authorities, the Red Cross, and the military. The scale of the destruction and the remote locations of many affected areas made these efforts challenging, but the response was swift and coordinated. Survivors were provided with temporary shelter, food, and medical care, while search teams combed the debris for victims and survivors. The community response was marked by acts of heroism and solidarity, as residents and volunteers worked tirelessly to aid those in need.

The collapse of the St. Francis Dam prompted an urgent and comprehensive investigation to determine the causes of the disaster and to prevent similar incidents in the future. A commission of inquiry was established by the state of California, led by a panel of experts in engineering and geology. The investigation revealed a series of critical failures and deficiencies in the design, construction, and oversight of the dam.

One of the primary findings was that the geological conditions at the dam site were fundamentally unsuitable for a large concrete structure. The underlying rock formations were highly fractured and prone to movement, which compromised the stability of the dam's foundation and abutments. The investigation also found that the design of the dam did not adequately account for the potential stresses and pressures exerted by the water in the reservoir. The use of concrete, while common at the time, was found to be inadequate for the conditions at the site, leading to cracks and seepage that weakened the structure.

Additionally, the investigation highlighted deficiencies in the oversight and management of the project. William Mulholland, despite his expertise and experience, had not conducted a thorough geological survey of the site, relying instead on visual inspections and assumptions about the suitability of the location. The project also lacked independent review and oversight, with decisions being made by a small team without external input or validation. These shortcomings reflected broader issues in the practices and standards of civil engineering at the time.

The findings of the investigation had profound implications for the field of civil engineering and public policy. One of the immediate outcomes was the resignation of William Mulholland, who took full responsibility for the disaster. Mulholland, who had been a celebrated figure in the development of Los Angeles' water infrastructure, retired in disgrace and spent the remaining years of his life reflecting on the tragedy. His fall from grace underscored the personal and professional consequences of engineering failures.

The St. Francis Dam disaster also led to significant changes in engineering practices and regulatory standards. One of the most important outcomes was the establishment of more rigorous standards for dam design, construction, and maintenance. The state of California enacted new regulations requiring comprehensive geological surveys and independent reviews for all major infrastructure projects. These measures were aimed at ensuring that the lessons learned from the St. Francis Dam failure would be applied to prevent similar tragedies in the future.

Additionally, the disaster prompted the development of new engineering techniques and technologies for assessing and managing the risks associated with large dams. Advances in geology, materials science, and structural engineering were incorporated into the design and construction of dams, leading to safer and more reliable infrastructure. The field of civil engineering as a whole became more rigorous and scientific, with a greater emphasis on empirical evidence and independent validation.

The legacy of the St. Francis Dam failure extends beyond the immediate changes in engineering practices and regulations. The disaster has become a symbol of the potential consequences of engineering failures and the importance of accountability, oversight, and continuous improvement in the field of civil engineering. The lessons learned from the collapse continue to inform the design and management of infrastructure projects around the world, ensuring that the tragic events of March 12, 1928, are not forgotten.

Memorials and commemorations have been established to honor the victims of the St. Francis Dam disaster and to educate future generations about the importance of engineering safety. The site of the dam, now a barren and silent canyon, serves as a poignant reminder of the human and material costs of engineering failures. Annual ceremonies and educational programs ensure that the memory of the disaster is preserved and that the lessons learned continue to be applied to prevent future tragedies.

Epilogue

As we reach the end of this journey through history's most consequential errors, it is essential to pause and reflect on the lessons these stories impart. Each chapter in "Minor Error, Major Consequences: True Stories of Unexpected Impacts" has showcased how a single misstep, often minor and seemingly insignificant, can trigger a cascade of events leading to profound and sometimes tragic outcomes. These incidents serve as powerful reminders of our vulnerability to error and the importance of vigilance in all aspects of life.

Throughout this book, we have traversed the globe and spanned centuries, witnessing the catastrophic effects of human oversight, misjudgment, and negligence. From the fiery destruction of the Hindenburg to the quiet, insidious buildup of toxic waste in Love Canal, each story is a testament to the complexity and interconnectedness of our world. These tragedies are not just historical footnotes; they are poignant lessons etched into the fabric of our shared human experience.

One of the most striking themes emerging from these narratives is the unpredictability of consequences. The margin between safety and disaster is often razor-thin, with small decisions or oversights having the potential to set off a chain reaction of unintended effects. This inherent unpredictability underscores the need for a culture of safety, meticulous planning, and continuous learning. It reminds us that diligence and attention to detail are not mere formalities but critical safeguards against potential catastrophe.

Another profound takeaway from these stories is the resilience and ingenuity that often follow disaster. Human beings have an extraordinary capacity to learn from mistakes, adapt, and innovate. Many of the incidents chronicled in this book led to significant changes in regulations, technologies, and practices aimed at preventing similar occurrences in the future. The suffering and loss endured by those affected by these tragedies were not in vain; their stories have spurred advancements that continue to save lives and protect communities.

As we close this book, we must carry forward the knowledge and wisdom gleaned from these stories. In our personal and professional lives, we must strive to recognize the potential impact of our actions, however small, and foster an environment where mistakes are not just acknowledged but rigorously analyzed and learned from. By embracing a mindset of continuous improvement and accountability, we can honor the memory of those who suffered from past errors and work towards a safer, more conscientious future.

"Minor Error, Major Consequences" is more than a collection of cautionary tales; it is a call to action. It implores us to remain ever-vigilant, to value precision and care, and to never underestimate the far-reaching effects of our decisions. As we move forward, let us carry these lessons with us, ever mindful of the thin line between routine and disaster, and ever committed to making choices that safeguard the well-being of all.

May these stories serve as both a warning and an inspiration, guiding us to create a world where minor errors are recognized and corrected before they can lead to major consequences.

The End.